This Book Belongs To:

Christmas 2011

2011 Christmas

with Southern Living

2011
Christmas
with Southern Living®

Oxmoor
House®

ISBN-13: 978-0-8487-3463-3
ISBN-10: 0-8487-3463-7
ISSN: 0747-7791
Printed in the United States of America
First Printing 2011

Oxmoor House
VP, Publishing Director: Jim Childs
Editorial Director: Susan Payne Dobbs
Brand Manager: Daniel Fagan
Senior Editor: Rebecca Brennan
Managing Editor: Laurie S. Herr

Christmas with Southern Living 2011

Editor: Katherine Cobbs
Project Editor: Emily Chappell
Director, Test Kitchens: Elizabeth Tyler Austin
Assistant Directors, Test Kitchens: Julie Christopher, Julie Gunter
Test Kitchens Professionals: Wendy Ball, Allison E. Cox, Victoria E. Cox, Margaret Monroe Dickey, Alyson Moreland Haynes, Stefanie Maloney, Callie Nash, Kathleen Royal Phillips, Catherine Crowell Steele, Leah Van Deren
Photography Director: Jim Bathie
Senior Photo Stylist: Kay E. Clarke
Associate Photo Stylist: Katherine Eckert Coyne
Assistant Photo Stylist: Mary Louise Menendez
Senior Production Manager: Greg A. Amason

Contributors
Designer: Carol Damsky
Copy Editor: Donna Baldone
Proofreader: Adrienne Davis
Indexer: Mary Ann Laurens
Interns: Alison Loughman, Caitlin Watzke
Photographers: Mary Britton Senseney, Becky Luigart-Stayner, Jason Wallis
Photo Stylists: Susan Huff, Mindi Shapiro-Levine, Sara Gae Waters

Southern Living
Editor: Lindsay Bierman
Executive Editor: Rachel Hardage
Food Director: Shannon Sliter Satterwhite
Test Kitchen Director: Rebecca Kracke Gordon
Senior Writer: Donna Florio
Senior Food Editors: Shirley Harrington, Mary Allen Perry
Recipe Editor: JoAnn Weatherly
Assistant Recipe Editor: Ashley Arthur
Test Kitchen Specialists/Food Styling: Marian Cooper Cairns, Vanessa McNeil Rocchio
Test Kitchen Professionals: Norman King, Pam Lolley, Angela Sellers
Travel Editors: James T. Black, Kim Cross
Features Editor: Jennifer V. Cole
Associate Travel Editor: Alex Crevar
Senior Photographers: Ralph Anderson, Gary Clark, Jennifer Davick, Art Meripol
Photographer: Robbie Caponetto
Photo Research Coordinator: Ginny P. Allen
Senior Photo Stylist: Buffy Hargett
Editorial Assistant: Pat York

To order additional publications, call 1-800-765-6400 or 1-800-491-0551.

For more books to enrich your life, visit **oxmoorhouse.com**

To search, savor, and share thousands of recipes, visit **myrecipes.com**

Cover: Strawberry-Pecan Icebox Cookies (page 33), German Chocolate Cake Truffles (page 116), Black and White Peppermint Fudge (page 154), Not Your Grandma's Divinity (page 158)

Back Cover: Christmas Tree Wreath (page 91), Spiked Apricot-Cranberry Sauce (page 108), Merry Mantel (page 66)

*W*elcome

This year's edition of Christmas with Southern Living is brimming with holiday inspiration. Whether you're planning to make handcrafted confections to share, holiday meals to remember, or creative crafts to give, you'll find more than 100 new recipes and a sleighful of decorating ideas and projects to keep your home humming with merry activity right through the New Year.

We show you how to deck the halls with flea market finds and collections you may have on hand, combining them in whimsical displays that say "Merry Christmas" in unexpected ways. Need ideas for displaying all those Christmas cards you receive? How about new approaches to gift wrap? We've got it all. This year we've designed 10 homemade gifts that are certain to bring a smile to every person on your gift list.

We hope this edition enriches your holiday. Thank you for letting us share it with you.

Wishing you an enchanted Christmas season,

Katherine Cobbs
Editor

CONTENTS

Entertain

THE HOUSE IS DRESSED FOR THE HOLIDAYS
AND THE FIRE IS LIT, IT'S TIME TO OPEN
THE DOOR TO A SEASON OF CELEBRATION
WITH FAMILY AND FRIENDS.

Daybreak
IN DIXIE

Family arrives from all directions both near and
far to gather together to celebrate the season.
Catch up over a sit-down breakfast
fit for a king.

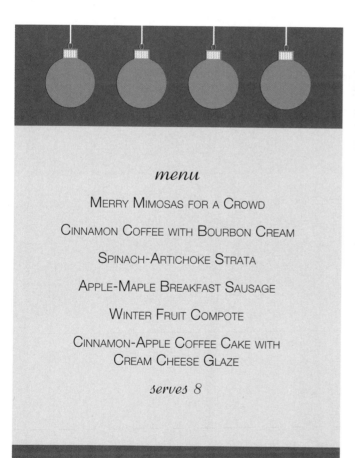

menu

MERRY MIMOSAS FOR A CROWD

CINNAMON COFFEE WITH BOURBON CREAM

SPINACH-ARTICHOKE STRATA

APPLE-MAPLE BREAKFAST SAUSAGE

WINTER FRUIT COMPOTE

CINNAMON-APPLE COFFEE CAKE WITH
CREAM CHEESE GLAZE

serves 8

Merry Mimosas for a Crowd

Makes 7 cups • Hands-On Time: 5 min. • Total Time: 5 min.

We put a festive twist on the traditional mimosa by adding a splash
of cranberry juice.

 3 cups fresh orange juice, chilled
 1 cup cranberry juice cocktail, chilled
 1 (750-milliliter) bottle Champagne or sparkling wine,
    chilled
Garnishes: frozen cranberries

1. Combine orange juice and cranberry juice in a large pitcher.
Add Champagne just before serving. Garnish, if desired. Serve
immediately.

Note: Mimosas can be made 1 at a time by stirring together
orange juice and cranberry juice, and then pouring equal parts
orange juice mixture and Champagne into champagne flutes.

Spinach-Artichoke
Strata

Apple-Maple Breakfast
Sausage

GAME PLAN

2 days before:
- Chill juices and Champagne.
- Prepare compote; cover and chill.

1 day before:
- Assemble strata; cover and chill unbaked.
- Set up coffee maker.
- Make sausage patties; cover and chill.
- Prepare coffee cake; store at room temperature.

1½ hours before:
- Bake strata; let stand.

45 minutes before:
- Prepare Bourbon Cream; cover and chill.

30 minutes before:
- Bring compote to room temperature.
- Brew coffee.

20 minutes before:
- Fry sausage patties.

15 minutes before:
- Stir together mimosa, and garnish.

Cinnamon Coffee with Bourbon Cream

Makes 8 cups • Hands-On Time: 11 min. • Total Time: 21 min.

Aromatic cinnamon will fill the air as this coffee brews.

- 1 cup medium-roast ground coffee
- 1 tsp. ground cinnamon
- 1 cup heavy cream
- 2 Tbsp. light brown sugar
- 2 Tbsp. bourbon
- Additional ground cinnamon
- 8 (3-inch) cinnamon sticks (optional)

1. Combine ground coffee and 1 tsp. cinnamon in a coffee filter. Brew coffee in a 12-cup coffeemaker according to manufacturer's instructions using 8 cups water.
2. Beat heavy cream at high speed with an electric mixer until foamy; add brown sugar, 1 Tbsp. at a time, beating until soft peaks form. Stir in bourbon. Chill until ready to serve.
3. Top each serving with bourbon cream, additional ground cinnamon, and, if desired, a cinnamon stick.

Note: 8 cups of water poured into a coffeemaker show as 12 cups in the coffeepot.

Spinach-Artichoke Strata

Makes 8 servings • Hands-On Time: 16 min. • Total Time: 9 hr., 36 min.

This crusty brunch dish delivers everything we love in the classic spinach-artichoke dip.

- 1½ (8-oz.) packages sliced fresh mushrooms
- 1 small onion, chopped (about 1¼ cups)
- 1 Tbsp. olive oil
- 1 (12-oz.) French or Italian bread loaf, torn into 1-inch pieces and divided
- 2 (6-oz.) packages fresh baby spinach
- 8 large eggs
- 3 cups milk
- 1 (8-oz.) container sour cream
- 1 tsp. dried Italian seasoning
- ¼ tsp. freshly ground pepper
- 2 (5-oz.) packages shredded Parmesan cheese, divided
- 1 cup (4 oz.) shredded mozzarella cheese
- 1 (14-oz.) can artichoke hearts, drained and chopped
- 1 (12-oz.) jar roasted red bell peppers, drained and chopped

1. Cook mushrooms and onion in oil in a large skillet over medium-high heat 8 to 10 minutes or until onion is tender.
2. Meanwhile, measure 1½ cups torn bread pieces, and place in a small food processor. Pulse bread 3 or 4 times to make coarse breadcrumbs; set aside.
3. Gradually add spinach to cooked mushroom mixture. Cook over medium-high heat, stirring constantly, just until spinach wilts. Remove from heat, and let cool slightly.
4. Whisk together eggs and next 4 ingredients in a large bowl. Stir in remaining bread pieces, 1½ packages Parmesan cheese, mozzarella cheese, artichokes, and bell peppers. Stir in mushroom mixture. Spoon into a greased 13- x 9-inch baking dish. Top with remaining Parmesan cheese and reserved breadcrumbs. Cover and chill 8 hours.
5. Preheat oven to 350°. Uncover strata, and bake at 350° for 1 hour and 20 minutes or until browned and set.

make ahead

Apple-Maple Breakfast Sausage

Makes 8 servings • Hands-On Time: 41 min. • Total Time: 1 hr., 41 min.

- 2 lb. ground pork
- 2 Tbsp. maple syrup
- 2 tsp. finely chopped fresh sage
- 1½ tsp. salt
- 1½ tsp. freshly ground pepper
- 1 Gala apple, peeled, cored, and finely chopped
- 1 Tbsp. canola oil

1. Combine first 6 ingredients in a large bowl. Shape mixture into 16 patties. Cover and chill at least 1 hour.
2. Heat oil a large skillet over medium-high heat. Cook patties, in 2 batches, 3 to 4 minutes on each side or until no longer pink.

Winter Fruit Compote

Makes 8 servings • Hands-On Time: 7 min. • Total Time: 37 min.

Dried fruit plumped with wine provides a great way to enjoy a colorful midwinter fruit dish.

- 1 cup sweet white wine
- ½ cup sugar
- 1 cup dried cherries
- 1 cup dried apricots
- ½ cup dried cranberries
- 1 (3-inch) cinnamon stick
- 2 Bosc pears, peeled and cut into 1-inch pieces
- ¼ tsp. almond extract
- 2 (8-oz.) containers plain yogurt
- ½ cup sliced almonds

1. Combine first 6 ingredients in a large saucepan; bring to a boil over medium-high heat. Reduce heat to medium-low; cover and simmer 15 minutes. Add pears, and simmer 15 more minutes or until pear is almost tender. Remove from heat; stir in extract. Discard cinnamon stick. Serve warm or at room temperature. Top each serving with a dollop of yogurt and 1 Tbsp. sliced almonds. (Compote can be prepared 2 days in advance and stored in refrigerator. Let stand 30 minutes before serving.)

Note: We tested with Riesling sweet white wine.

Winter Fruit Compote

Spinach-Artichoke Strata

Apple-Maple Breakfast Sausage

Cinnamon-Apple Coffee Cake
with Cream Cheese Glaze

editor's favorite ~ make ahead

Cinnamon-Apple Coffee Cake with Cream Cheese Glaze

Makes 8 to 10 servings • Hands-On Time: 50 min. • Total Time: 4 hr., 40 min., including streusel and glaze

This tall coffee cake is gooey good, packed with sour cream richness and cinnamon sugar.

- 1 cup peeled, finely chopped Golden Delicious apple
- ¾ cup finely chopped toasted walnuts
- ¼ cup firmly packed light brown sugar
- 1½ tsp. ground cinnamon
- 1 cup butter, softened
- 2 cups granulated sugar
- 2 large eggs
- 1 (8-oz.) container sour cream
- 2 tsp. vanilla extract
- 2 cups all-purpose flour
- 1 tsp. baking powder
- 1 tsp. ground cinnamon
- ½ tsp. salt
  Streusel Topping
  Cream Cheese Glaze

1. Preheat oven to 350°. Combine first 4 ingredients, stirring well; set aside.
2. Beat butter at medium speed with an electric mixer until creamy; gradually add granulated sugar, beating 3 to 5 minutes or until light and fluffy. Add eggs, 1 at a time, beating just until blended after each addition. Stir in sour cream and vanilla.
3. Combine flour, baking powder, 1 tsp. cinnamon, and salt; gradually add to butter mixture, beating at low speed just until blended. Spread half of batter into a greased and floured 9-inch springform pan. Spoon reserved apple mixture over batter to within ½-inch of edge. Spread remaining batter over apple mixture. Sprinkle with Streusel Topping.
4. Bake at 350° for 1 hour and 25 to 30 minutes or until a wooden pick inserted in center comes out clean. Let cool in pan on a wire rack 10 minutes. Remove sides of pan; let cool completely (about 1½ hours). Drizzle with Cream Cheese Glaze.

Streusel Topping

Makes about 1½ cups • Hands-On Time: 8 min. • Total Time: 8 min.

- ½ cup all-purpose flour
- ⅓ cup firmly packed light brown sugar
- 1 tsp. ground cinnamon
- ⅓ cup cold butter, cut into pieces
- ¾ cup chopped walnuts

1. Combine first 3 ingredients in a medium bowl; cut in butter with a pastry blender or fork until crumbly. Stir in walnuts.

Cream Cheese Glaze

Makes about 1 cup • Hands-On Time: 5 min. • Total Time: 5 min.

- 1 (3-oz.) package cream cheese, softened
- 1 tsp. vanilla extract
- 1½ cups powdered sugar
- 3 to 4 Tbsp. milk

1. Beat cream cheese at medium speed until creamy; add vanilla, beating well. Gradually add powdered sugar, beating at low speed just until blended. Gradually add enough milk to reach desired consistency.

Instead of studded pomanders, citrus is tied in matching ribbon for a pretty centerpiece.

Thanksgiving
FAMILY STYLE

By a blazing fire on the screened porch, Thanksgiving signals the start of the holiday season.

menu

GINGER CIDER

SEAFOOD APPETIZER TRIO

TURKEY BREAST WITH GRITS-MUSHROOM DRESSING

GREEN BEANS WITH FRIED SHALLOTS

TRIPLE-CHEESE BAKED MASHED POTATOES

GLAZED VEGETABLES WITH PARSLEY

PECAN PIE COBBLER WITH HONEY ICE CREAM

SWEET POTATO CAKE WITH ORANGE-CREAM CHEESE FROSTING

serves 8

GAME PLAN

2 days before:
- Make cake layers; wrap airtightly and freeze.
- Make grits for dressing; cover and chill.

1 day before:
- Make sauces for seafood; cover and chill.
- Cook shrimp; cover and chill.
- Prepare turkey; roll, tie, cover, and chill.
- Assemble potatoes in 13- x 9-inch baking dish; cover and chill. (Or prepare in slow cooker the following day.)
- Make ice cream; cover and freeze.
- Make cake frosting; frost and garnish cake. Cover and chill.

2 hours before:
- Remove turkey rolls from fridge; let stand for 30 minutes.

1½ hours before:
- Bake turkey.
- Prepare pecan pie cobbler.
- Bake potato casserole.

30 minutes before:
- Make gravy.
- Cook vegetable medley.
- Microwave beans, and fry shallots.
- Make cider.
- Broil oysters.

15 minutes before:
- Arrange seafood platter.

 make ahead

Ginger Cider

Makes 9 cups • Hands-On Time: 5 min. • Total Time: 17 min.

1 (64-oz.) bottle apple cider
2 cups pineapple juice
1 Tbsp. grated fresh ginger
1 vanilla bean, split lengthwise
1 (3-inch) cinnamon stick, broken
6 black peppercorns

1. Stir together first 3 ingredients in a large Dutch oven. Scrape vanilla bean seeds into cider mixture; add vanilla bean pod, cinnamon stick pieces, and peppercorns. Bring to a simmer over medium-high heat; reduce heat to low. Keep warm until ready to serve.
2. Before serving, pour cider through a wire-mesh strainer into a serving bowl, discarding solids.

 make ahead

Seafood Appetizer Trio

Makes 10 to 12 servings • Hands-On Time: 40 min. • Total Time: 1 hr., 57 min., including sauces

Just to be on the safe side, we give you cooking directions for oysters on the half shell rather than serving them raw. All crab is cooked when you purchase it. The smaller blue crab is most readily available and loved in the South, but for a more dramatic show on the plate, purchase frozen Alaskan Snow crab, which comes in a cluster. Just break it apart.

1½ lb. unpeeled, large raw shrimp with tails (31/35 count)
2 dozen fresh oysters in the shell
  Rock salt
2 lb. crab claws
  Lemon wedges
  Saltine crackers
  Hot sauce
  Triple Threat Mignonette
  Bloody Mary Cocktail Sauce
  Orange-Cilantro Butter Sauce
  Lemon-Caper Rémoulade

1. Bring 3 qt. water to a boil; add shrimp, and cook 3 to 5 minutes or just until shrimp turn pink. Drain and rinse with cold water. Chill.
2. Preheat broiler with oven rack 3 inches from heat. Scrub oysters with a stiff brush under running water. Insert an oyster knife into the hinged edge of each oyster; twist knife handle back and forth until top shell is loose. Slide oyster knife along the bottom of the shell to detach muscle. Remove and discard top shell; keep oysters in the deeper bottom shell. Arrange oysters over rock salt in a jelly-roll pan. Broil 2 to 3 minutes or until edges begin to curl. (Serve oysters hot, but other seafood should be served chilled.)
3. Arrange seafood on a large serving platter. Serve with lemon wedges, crackers, hot sauce, and desired sauces.

Lemon-Caper Rémoulade

Bloody Mary
Cocktail Sauce

Triple Threat
Mignonelle

Seafood Appetizer Trio

Orange-Cilantro Butter
Sauce

Triple Threat Mignonette

(pictured on page 21)
Makes ¾ cup • Hands-On Time: 5 min. • Total Time: 59 min.

1 cup dry white wine
¼ cup sherry vinegar
2 large shallots, minced
2 tsp. mixed peppercorns, crushed
¼ tsp. kosher salt

1. Combine first 3 ingredients in a small saucepan. Cook over medium-high heat 22 minutes or until reduced to ¾ cup. Remove from heat; stir in peppercorns and salt. Let cool completely (about 32 minutes). Cover and chill until ready to serve.

Bloody Mary Cocktail Sauce

(pictured on page 21)
Makes 1⅓ cups • Hands-On Time: 5 min. • Total Time: 5 min.

1 cup ketchup
3 Tbsp. vodka
2 Tbsp. refrigerated horseradish
1 Tbsp. Worcestershire sauce
1 Tbsp. fresh lemon juice
¼ teaspoon celery seeds
2 garlic cloves, minced

1. Combine all ingredients in a small bowl. Cover and chill until ready to serve.

Orange-Cilantro Butter Sauce

(pictured on page 21)
Makes 1¼ cups • Hands-On Time: 5 min. • Total Time: 26 min.

2 cups dry white wine
½ cup fresh orange juice
2 Tbsp. white wine vinegar
3 large garlic cloves, minced
½ cup whipping cream
½ cup butter, cut into pieces
½ cup chopped fresh cilantro
1 tsp. orange zest

1. Bring first 4 ingredients to a boil in a medium saucepan over medium-high heat. Cook 15 minutes or until mixture is reduced to ¼ cup. Stir in cream. Reduce heat to medium-low; simmer 3 minutes or until thickened.
2. Reduce heat to low. Add butter, 1 Tbsp. at a time, whisking until butter is melted and sauce is thickened. Remove from heat; stir in cilantro and zest.

Lemon-Caper Rémoulade

(pictured on page 21)
Makes 1¼ cups • Hands-On Time: 6 min. • Total Time: 6 min.

¾ cup mayonnaise
¼ cup whole grain mustard
2 Tbsp. chopped capers
2 Tbsp. minced green onion
2 Tbsp. finely chopped fresh parsley
1 Tbsp. chili sauce
1 Tbsp. fresh lemon juice

1. Combine all ingredients in a small bowl. Cover and chill until ready to serve.

Note: Toss any leftover rémoulade sauce with cooked shrimp for a light seafood salad.

editor's favorite ~ make ahead

Turkey Breast with Grits-Mushroom Dressing

Makes 12 servings • Hands-On Time: 1 hr., 11 min. • Total Time: 4 hr., 55 min.

Butterfly and stuff two boneless turkey breasts with this Southern-style grits dressing. Bake them side by side and thinly slice servings.

3 cups chicken broth
1 cup uncooked quick-cooking grits
3 applewood-smoked bacon slices
1 (8-oz.) package baby portobello mushrooms, coarsely chopped
½ cup chopped onion
2 celery ribs, chopped
2 garlic cloves, minced
2 Tbsp. chopped fresh sage
2 (3-lb.) skinned and boned turkey breasts
3 Tbsp. butter, melted
1½ tsp. salt
½ tsp. freshly ground pepper
¼ cup all-purpose flour
2 cups chicken broth
2 Tbsp. whipping cream

1. Combine 3 cups broth and grits in a large saucepan; bring to a boil over medium-high heat, stirring constantly. Cover, reduce heat, and simmer 5 minutes or until thickened. Remove from heat; pour grits into a greased 8-inch square pan. Cool completely. Cover and chill grits 2 hours or until very firm. Grits can be covered and chilled up to 2 days, if desired.

Triple-Cheese Baked Mashed Potatoes

Glazed Vegetables with Parsley

Turkey Breast with Grits-Mushroom Dressing

2. Preheat oven to 450°. Invert chilled grits onto a cutting board; remove pan. Cut grits into ¾-inch croutons. Place grits croutons in a single layer on a large greased baking sheet or jelly-roll pan. Bake at 450° for 20 minutes; turn grits, and bake 12 more minutes or until crisp and browned. Set aside. Reduce oven temperature to 400°.

3. Cook bacon in a large skillet over medium heat 8 minutes or until crisp; remove bacon, and drain on paper towels, reserving drippings in skillet. Crumble bacon, and set aside.

4. Sauté mushrooms, onion, and celery in drippings in skillet 5 minutes. Add garlic; sauté 1 more minute. Remove from heat; stir in chopped sage. Combine grits croutons, sautéed vegetables, and crumbled bacon in a bowl; set aside.

5. Butterfly turkey breasts by making a lengthwise cut in 1 side of each breast, cutting to but not through the opposite side; unfold. Place each breast between 2 sheets of heavy-duty plastic wrap, and flatten to ½-inch thickness, using a rolling pin or the flat side of a meat mallet.

6. Working with 1 breast at a time, brush 1 side of breast with 1 Tbsp. melted butter; sprinkle both sides with ¾ tsp. salt and

¼ tsp. pepper. Spoon 2 cups grits mixture over buttered side of breast, leaving a 2-inch border. Roll up, starting at 1 long side. Tie with kitchen string, securing at 2-inch intervals. Place turkey roll, seam side down, in a lightly greased roasting pan. Repeat procedure with remaining turkey breast, 1 Tbsp. butter, ¾ tsp. salt, ¼ tsp. pepper, and grits mixture. Place turkey roll, seam side down, several inches apart, on same pan. Brush both rolls with remaining 1 Tbsp. melted butter.

7. Bake at 400° for 45 to 55 minutes or until a meat thermometer inserted into thickest portion registers 170°. Remove from oven; let stand 10 minutes before slicing.

8. Transfer pan drippings to a saucepan, if desired, or continue cooking in roasting pan placed over 2 burners on the stovetop. Whisk together flour and 2 cups broth; add to drippings in pan, whisking until blended. Bring to a boil over medium-high heat, whisking constantly. Cook 3 to 5 minutes or until gravy is thickened. Whisk in cream.

9. Slice turkey rolls, and arrange slices on a serving platter. Serve with gravy.

Green Beans with Fried Shallots

Makes 10 to 12 servings • Hands-On Time: 6 min. • Total Time: 14 min.

Golden fried shallot rings add pleasing texture to these beans.

2½ lb. fresh green beans, trimmed
 2 Tbsp. butter
 1 tsp. salt, divided
 1 tsp. freshly ground pepper, divided
 ¼ cup olive oil
 4 shallots, thinly sliced and separated into rings
 1 Tbsp. all-purpose flour
 3 large garlic cloves, thinly sliced
1½ Tbsp. fresh lemon juice

1. Place beans and ½ cup water in a large microwave-safe bowl. Cover with plastic wrap; fold back a small edge to allow steam to escape. Microwave at HIGH 8 minutes or until beans are crisp-tender; drain well, and return to bowl. Add butter; sprinkle with ¾ tsp. each salt and pepper. Stir until butter melts. Cover and keep warm.
2. Heat oil in a large skillet over medium-high heat. Toss shallots with flour in a small bowl. Sauté shallots in hot oil 2 to 3 minutes or just until sizzling and crisp; remove shallots with a slotted spoon, and drain on paper towels. Sprinkle with remaining ¼ tsp. each salt and pepper. Add garlic to oil in skillet; sauté 20 to 30 seconds or just until fragrant. Remove from heat; pour garlic and oil over reserved beans. Sprinkle with lemon juice, and top with fried shallots.

Fix It Faster: Substitute 3 (12-oz.) packages ready-to-eat trimmed fresh green beans for the fresh green beans, omitting water. Pierce bags with a fork, and microwave at HIGH 4 to 5 minutes or until crisp-tender. Proceed with recipe as directed.

 *editor's favorite ~ make ahead*

Triple-Cheese Baked Mashed Potatoes

(pictured on page 23)

Makes 12 servings • Hands-On Time: 23 min. • Total Time: 1 hr., 16 min.

The rich, buttery flavor and creamy texture of these potatoes will please a crowd.

 5 lb. Yukon gold potatoes, peeled and cut into 1-inch cubes
 1 tsp. salt
 1 (6- or 8-oz.) Gouda or Edam cheese round, shredded
 1 cup freshly grated Parmesan cheese, divided
 ½ cup butter, melted and divided
 ½ tsp. salt
 1 (8-oz.) package cream cheese, softened
 1 (8-oz.) container sour cream
 ¾ cup fresh French breadcrumbs

1. Preheat oven to 350°. Bring potatoes, 1 tsp. salt, and water to cover to a boil in a large Dutch oven over medium-high heat, and cook 20 to 25 minutes or until tender. Drain potatoes, and return to pan. Mash potatoes with a masher to desired consistency.
2. Meanwhile, stir together Gouda cheese, ¾ cup Parmesan, ⅓ cup melted butter, ½ tsp. salt, cream cheese, and sour cream. Add to mashed potatoes, stirring until smooth.
3. Spoon potato mixture into a greased 13- x 9-inch baking dish. Combine breadcrumbs, remaining ¼ cup Parmesan cheese, and remaining melted butter in a small bowl; sprinkle over potatoes.
4. Bake, uncovered, at 350° for 40 minutes or until bubbly and lightly browned. Let stand 5 minutes.

Note: Potatoes will be creamiest if mashed alone with a potato ricer or potato masher before adding other ingredients.

Slow Cooker Triple-Cheese Mashed Potatoes:
Prepare recipe as directed above through step 2. Spoon potato mixture into a lightly greased 5-qt. slow cooker. Cover and cook on LOW 3 hours. Meanwhile, combine breadcrumbs, ¼ cup Parmesan cheese, and remaining melted butter; spread on a baking sheet. Bake at 350° for 8 minutes; sprinkle over potatoes before serving.

Pecan Pie Cobbler
with Honey Ice Cream

quick & easy

Glazed Vegetables with Parsley

(pictured on page 23)
Makes 10 to 12 servings • Hands-On Time: 13 min. • Total Time: 28 min.

Look for tender young parsnips in the produce department. They're readily available in the winter months, they cook up fast, and offer a naturally sweet flavor to this dish.

- ¼ cup unsalted butter
- ½ cup chicken or vegetable broth
- 1½ Tbsp. brown sugar
- 1 lb. parsnips, peeled and cut into ¾-inch-thick slices
- 1 lb. fresh Brussels sprouts, trimmed and halved
- ½ lb. carrots, cut into ¾-inch-thick slices
- 2 small red onions, each cut into 8 wedges
- Parchment paper
- ⅓ cup chopped fresh flat-leaf parsley
- Salt and freshly ground pepper to taste

1. Melt butter in a large deep skillet over medium-high heat. Add broth and brown sugar; cook 1 to 2 minutes or until sugar dissolves. Add parsnips and next 3 ingredients, stirring gently.
2. Cut out a round of parchment paper (or aluminum foil, if necessary) to fit snugly in skillet; place paper directly onto vegetables, and cover with lid. Cook over medium heat 12 to 13 minutes or until vegetables are tender and most of liquid evaporates.
3. Uncover, discard paper, and cook vegetables 1 to 2 minutes or just until glazed. Remove from heat; sprinkle with parsley. Season with salt and pepper to taste.

editor's favorite

Pecan Pie Cobbler with Honey Ice Cream

Makes 12 servings • Hands-On Time: 15 min. • Total Time: 1 hr., 4 min.

Pecan pie meets cobbler crust with a scoop of honey-laced ice cream on top. This combo says holiday like you've never tasted before.

- 2½ cups light corn syrup
- 2½ cups firmly packed light brown sugar
- ½ cup butter, melted
- 1½ Tbsp. vanilla extract
- 6 large eggs, lightly beaten
- 2 cups coarsely chopped pecans
- 1 (14.1-oz.) package refrigerated piecrusts
- Butter-flavored cooking spray
- 2 cups pecan halves
- Honey Ice Cream

1. Preheat oven to 425°. Combine first 5 ingredients in a large bowl, stirring with a whisk. Stir in coarsely chopped pecans.
2. Unroll 1 piecrust. Roll into a 13- x 9-inch rectangle. Trim sides to fit pan. Place pastry in a greased 13- x 9-inch baking dish. Spoon half of filling mixture into pastry. Unroll remaining piecrust. Roll into a 13- x 9-inch rectangle. Trim sides to fit pan. Place over filling in pan. Coat with cooking spray.
3. Bake at 425° for 14 to 16 minutes or until browned. Reduce oven temperature to 350°.
4. Carefully spoon remaining filling over baked pastry; arrange pecan halves on top in a decorative fashion. Bake at 350° for 30 minutes or until set. Cool 20 minutes on a wire rack; serve warm with Honey Ice Cream.

Sweet Potato Cake with Orange-Cream Cheese Frosting

Ginger Cider

Honey Ice Cream

(pictured on page 25)

Makes 7 cups • Hands-On Time: 4 min. • Total Time: 2 hr., 25 min.

- ¾ cup finely chopped pecans
- 3 Tbsp. butter, melted
- 6 cups vanilla ice cream
- ¼ cup honey

1. Preheat oven to 350°. Combine pecans and butter, stirring well. Spread in a single layer on a baking sheet. Bake at 350° for 10 minutes or until toasted. Cool completely.

2. Stir together toasted pecans, ice cream, and honey. Cover and freeze until firm.

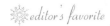
editor's favorite

Sweet Potato Cake with Orange-Cream Cheese Frosting

Makes 12 servings • Hands-On Time: 45 min. • Total Time: 2 hr., 20 min., including frosting

- Wax paper
- ½ cup crushed pineapple
- 1 cup butter, softened
- 1 cup granulated sugar
- 1 cup firmly packed light brown sugar
- 3 large eggs
- 3 cups all-purpose flour
- 2 tsp. baking powder
- 1 tsp. baking soda
- 2 tsp. pumpkin pie spice
- ½ tsp. salt
- 1 cup buttermilk
- 2 cups mashed sweet potatoes
- ¾ cup chopped pecans, toasted
- ½ cup sweetened flaked coconut
- 1 tsp. vanilla extract
- Orange-Cream Cheese Frosting
- Garnishes: candied pecans, orange zest

1. Preheat oven to 350°. Grease 3 (9-inch) round cake pans with shortening; line pans with wax paper, and grease paper. Dust with flour, shaking out excess.

2. Drain and press pineapple between paper towels to remove excess moisture. Set pineapple aside.

3. Beat butter and sugars at medium speed with an electric mixer until fluffy. Add eggs, 1 at a time, beating just until yellow disappears.

4. Combine flour and next 4 ingredients; add to butter mixture alternately with buttermilk, beginning and ending with flour mixture. Beat at low speed until blended after each addition, stopping to scrape bowl as needed. Stir in reserved pineapple, sweet potatoes, and next 3 ingredients until blended. Pour batter into prepared pans.

5. Bake at 350° for 25 to 30 minutes or until a wooden pick inserted in center comes out clean. Cool in pans on wire racks 10 minutes; remove from pans to wire racks, and cool completely (about 1 hour). Cake layers can be wrapped and frozen up to 2 days, if desired.

6. Spread Orange-Cream Cheese Frosting between layers and on top and sides of cake. Garnish, if desired.

Orange-Cream Cheese Frosting

Makes 6 cups • Hands-On Time: 10 min. • Total Time: 10 min.

- 1 navel orange, cut into quarters
- 1½ (8-oz.) packages cream cheese, softened
- ¾ cup butter, softened
- 6 cups powdered sugar
- 1½ tsp. vanilla extract

1. Peel orange sections, removing any bitter white pith. Process cream cheese and butter in a food processor just until smooth. Add 3 orange sections; process 20 seconds or until mixture is smooth. (Reserve remaining orange section for another use.) Transfer cream cheese mixture to a mixing bowl; gradually add powdered sugar, beating at low speed until blended. Stir in vanilla.

Road Trip
TO GRANDMA'S

Make the trip home for the holidays as memorable as the main event. Enjoy a picnic in the pines with great make-ahead, portable dishes that trump anything you could get from a drive-through.

menu

ROSEMARY-SCENTED COLD CIDER

COLD SKILLET-FRIED CHICKEN

APPLE-CABBAGE SLAW

SWEET POTATO SALAD

CHAMELEON ICEBOX COOKIES

CARAMEL DROP-BANANA BREAD
TRIFLE DESSERT

serves 6

GAME PLAN

2 days before:

- Prepare cider, omitting ginger ale; cover and chill.

1 day before:

- Prepare chicken; cool, cover, and chill.
- Prepare sweet potato salad; cover and chill.
- Prepare slaw; cover and chill.
- Prepare trifle; cover and chill.
- Prepare cookies; store in airtight container.

30 minutes before the trip:

- Pack up, placing chilled items in a cooler.

Just before:

- Stir ginger ale into cider.

✳ make ahead

Rosemary-Scented Cold Cider

Makes 9½ cups • Hands-On Time: 5 min. • Total Time: 8 hr., 5 min.

Pick up a jug of fresh-pressed cider for optimum results with this refreshing drink.

- 5 cups apple cider
- 4 (4- to 5-inch) fresh rosemary sprigs
- 2 cups cranberry-apple juice drink, chilled
- 2 (12-oz.) cans ginger ale, chilled

1. Bring cider and 4 rosemary sprigs to a boil in a saucepan over medium-high heat. Reduce heat to medium-low; simmer 3 minutes. Remove from heat; let cool to room temperature. Cover and chill 8 to 24 hours. Remove and discard rosemary sprigs.
2. Combine cider and cranberry-apple drink in a pitcher or thermos. Add ginger ale just before serving.

Cold Skillet-Fried Chicken

Makes 4 to 6 servings • Hands-On Time: 11 min. • Total Time: 2 hr., 37 min.

Enjoy this crispy, well-seasoned chicken hot from the skillet at home, or cool and chill it, and nibble on the road to Grandma's.

- 2 cups buttermilk
- ¼ cup dill pickle juice
- 1 Tbsp. chopped fresh rosemary
- ½ tsp. paprika
- ¼ tsp. ground red pepper
- 2 garlic cloves, pressed
- 1 (4-lb.) cut-up whole chicken
- 1 cup self-rising flour
- 1 Tbsp. plus 1 tsp. seasoned salt
- 2 tsp. freshly ground black pepper

Peanut oil

1. Place 1 large zip-top plastic freezer bag inside another zip-top plastic freezer bag. Combine first 6 ingredients in the inside bag. Add chicken pieces, tossing to coat. Seal both bags, and chill at least 2 hours or overnight.
2. Remove chicken from marinade, discarding marinade. Combine flour, salt, and black pepper. Dredge chicken in flour mixture, shaking off excess.
3. Pour oil to depth of 1½ inches in a deep skillet or Dutch oven; heat to 350°. Add chicken, a few pieces at a time; cover and cook 6 minutes. Uncover chicken, and cook 9 minutes. Turn chicken; cover and cook 6 minutes. Uncover and cook 5 to 9 minutes, turning chicken the last 3 minutes for even browning, if necessary. Drain on paper towels. Serve immediately, or let cool; cover and chill.

Cold Skillet-Fried Chicken

Chameleon Icebox Cookies

Sweet Potato Salad

Apple-Cabbage Slaw

make ahead

Apple-Cabbage Slaw

Makes 8 to 10 servings • Hands-On Time: 5 min. • Total Time: 5 min.

Adding dried fruit and nut mix to this slaw is an easy way to add color, flavor, and crunch in a single ingredient.

- ½ cup canola oil
- 3 Tbsp. cider vinegar
- 2 Tbsp. honey
- ½ tsp. salt
- ⅛ tsp. pepper
- 1 (10-oz.) package finely shredded cabbage
- 1 cup dried fruit and nut mix
- 2 Fuji apples, cored and finely chopped
- 2 green onions, minced

1. Whisk together first 5 ingredients in a large bowl; add cabbage and remaining ingredients. Toss well. Cover and chill until ready to serve.

Sweet Potato Salad

Makes 6 to 8 servings • Hands-On Time: 11 min. • Total Time: 56 min.

This salad is great warm or chilled. With honey-mustard undertones, it pairs well with fried chicken, turkey, or ham.

- 4 large sweet potatoes, peeled and cubed
- 1 Tbsp. olive oil
- ½ tsp. salt
- ½ tsp. pepper
- 2 Tbsp. mustard seeds
- ¼ cup rice vinegar
- 3 Tbsp. honey
- ¼ tsp. ground cinnamon
- ¼ tsp. curry powder
- ¼ tsp. dry mustard

1. Preheat oven to 450°. Toss together sweet potatoes, oil, salt, and pepper on a lightly greased large rimmed baking sheet or roasting pan. Roast at 450° for 45 minutes or until potatoes are tender and lightly browned. (Do not stir.)
2. Meanwhile, toast mustard seeds in a small skillet over medium heat until fragrant, stirring or shaking skillet to prevent burning. Add vinegar, honey, and spices; bring to a boil. Remove from heat. Pour over sweet potatoes in a serving bowl; toss. Serve warm, or cover and chill.

great gift ~ make ahead

Chameleon Icebox Cookies

Makes about 4 dozen • Hands-On Time: 18 min. • Total Time: 49 min.

Old-fashioned icebox cookies become a creative and tasty blank canvas for Christmas stir-ins. Our staff had a hard time choosing a favorite variation.

- 1 cup butter, softened
- 1 cup superfine sugar
- 1 large egg
- 2 tsp. vanilla extract
- 2¼ cups all-purpose flour
- ½ tsp. salt
- Wax paper

1. Beat butter at medium speed with an electric mixer until creamy; gradually add sugar, beating well. Add egg and vanilla; beat well.
2. Combine flour and salt; add to butter mixture, beating at medium-low speed just until blended. Cover and chill dough at least 1 hour.
3. Shape dough into 2 (6-inch) logs. Wrap logs in wax paper or parchment paper; chill or freeze until firm.
4. Preheat oven to 350°. Slice dough into ¼-inch-thick slices. Place on ungreased baking sheets. Bake at 350° for 12 minutes or until barely golden. Remove to wire racks, and let cool completely (about 10 minutes).

Bittersweet Chocolate & Orange Essence Icebox Cookies: Stir ½ cup (4 oz.) finely chopped bittersweet chocolate and 1 Tbsp. orange zest into dough. Proceed with recipe as directed. Bake 12 to 13 minutes or until golden.

Strawberry-Pecan Icebox Cookies: Stir ¾ cup finely chopped dried strawberries into dough. Roll logs in 1 cup finely chopped pecans. Proceed with recipe as directed.

Kids' Icebox Cookies: Roll 1 log of dough in ⅓ cup green decorator sugar crystals. Roll remaining log in ⅓ cup red decorator sugar crystals. Proceed with recipe as directed.

Lavender Icebox Cookies: Stir 1½ Tbsp. dried lavender, lightly crushed, into dough. Proceed with recipe as directed.
Note: We used a mini food chopper to crush the lavender.

Caramel Drop-Banana Bread
Trifle Dessert

make ahead

Caramel Drop-Banana Bread Trifle Dessert

Makes 8 to 10 servings • Hands-On Time: 30 min. • Total Time: 2 hr.

Instead of using vanilla wafers in this yummy banana pudding dessert, we chopped a loaf of banana bread. Pick up a loaf at a local bakery or grocer's bakery section. Assemble this dessert in a large, shallow plastic container with a lid; chill and take it to a holiday gathering.

CUSTARD

- 1 cup sugar
- ⅔ cup all-purpose flour
- ½ tsp. salt
- 5 cups milk
- 5 egg yolks
- 1 Tbsp. vanilla extract
- 1 Tbsp. butter

TRIFLE DESSERT

- 1 (1-lb.) banana bread loaf without nuts (about 8 x 4 inches)
- 2 large ripe bananas, sliced
- 1 (13.4-oz.) can dulce de leche
- 1 (8-oz.) container frozen whipped topping, thawed
- 1 cup chopped pecans, toasted

1. Prepare Custard: Combine first 3 ingredients in a heavy saucepan; whisk in milk. Cook over medium heat, stirring constantly, until thickened and bubbly (about 12 minutes).
2. Whisk egg yolks until thick and pale. Gradually stir about one-fourth of hot mixture into yolks; add yolk mixture to remaining hot mixture, stirring constantly. Cook over medium heat, stirring gently, 3 minutes. Remove from heat; add vanilla and butter, stirring until butter melts. Cool to room temperature. Cover and chill up to a day ahead. (Custard will be thick.)
3. Prepare Trifle Dessert: Chop banana bread loaf into ¾-inch pieces to yield about 5 cups. Place banana bread pieces in a 13- x 9-inch baking dish or similar size heavy-duty plastic container. Spoon and spread Custard over banana bread; top with banana slices. Top dessert with small dollops of dulce de leche. Top with whipped topping, spreading to edges; sprinkle with pecans. Cover and chill 1 to 24 hours.

Vintage SOUTHERN HOLIDAY

Set the table with your most prized family heirlooms and celebrate the holidays with this elegant meal of Southern classics.

menu

SPIKED SATSUMA CHAMPAGNE

PICKLED SHRIMP

FIELD GREENS WITH COUNTRY-HAM CORNBREAD CROUTONS
AND MUSCADINE VINAIGRETTE

PECAN SOUP

CROWN PORK ROAST WITH BOURBON-CARAMELIZED
ONIONS AND APPLES

WHITE CHEESE GRITS WITH MUSTARD GREENS AND BACON

BROWNED BUTTER-GLAZED CARROTS

CARAMEL-PEAR CAKE

serves 8

GAME PLAN

1 day before:
- Make simple syrup for Champagne; cover and chill. Freeze orange slices.
- Prepare pickled shrimp; cover and chill.
- Prepare croutons for salad; cover.
- Prepare vinaigrette for salad; cover and chill.
- Bake cake layers, and drizzle with syrup; cover and chill overnight.

Morning of:
- Fill and frost cake.

3½ hours before:
- Assemble and bake pork roast.

1½ hours before:
- Prepare soup; keep warm.

1 hour before:
- Prepare carrots.

45 minutes before:
- Prepare grits dish; keep warm.

20 minutes before:
- Prepare and plate salads.

Just before:
- Assemble beverage.
- Stir parsley into shrimp.

Spiked Satsuma Champagne

editor's favorite

Spiked Satsuma Champagne

Makes 9½ cups • Hands-On Time: 13 min. • Total Time: 43 min.

Frozen orange slices serve double duty as ice cubes and garnish in this bubbly elixir.

> 2 satsumas, thinly sliced
> Wax paper
> ½ cup sugar
> 2 cups fresh satsuma orange juice* (about 9 satsumas)
> ½ cup orange liqueur
> 2 (750-milliliter) bottles chilled dry Champagne

1. Arrange orange slices on a baking sheet lined with wax paper; freeze 30 minutes.

2. Combine ½ cup water and sugar in a 2-cup glass measuring cup. Microwave at HIGH 1 minute or until very hot. Stir until sugar dissolves.

3. Combine sugar syrup, juice, and liqueur in a pitcher; chill until ready to serve.

4. Place 1 frozen orange slice in each Champagne glass. Pour ¼ cup juice mixture into each glass. Top with Champagne, and serve immediately.

*Bottled tangerine juice may be substituted. Look for it in the produce section.

Pickled Shrimp

✳️ *make ahead*

Pickled Shrimp

Makes 12 servings • Hands-On Time: 20 min. • Total Time: 8 hr., 20 min.

Use decorative picks to serve these well-seasoned, piquant shrimp.

- 2 lb. unpeeled, large raw shrimp (26/30 count)
- 3 large garlic cloves, sliced
- 3 bay leaves
- 2 large lemons, thinly sliced
- 1 small red onion, thinly sliced
- ½ cup olive oil
- ¼ cup white wine vinegar
- 2 Tbsp. Old Bay seasoning
- 2 Tbsp. drained capers
- 1 Tbsp. whole black peppercorns
- 1 Tbsp. Worcestershire sauce
- 1 Tbsp. hot sauce
- 2 tsp. kosher salt
- 1 tsp. sugar
- ½ tsp. dried crushed red pepper
- ¼ cup chopped fresh parsley

1. Peel shrimp; devein, if desired. Cook shrimp in boiling water to cover 3 to 5 minutes or just until shrimp turn pink; drain. Rinse with cold water.

2. Combine shrimp and next 4 ingredients in a large bowl. Whisk together oil and next 9 ingredients; pour over shrimp mixture. Cover and chill 8 hours, stirring occasionally. Remove and discard bay leaves. Stir in parsley just before serving.

✳️ *editor's favorite ~ make ahead*

Field Greens with Country-Ham Cornbread Croutons and Muscadine Vinaigrette

Makes 12 servings • Hands-On Time: 7 min. • Total Time: 2 hr., including croutons and vinaigrette

A homemade sweet vinaigrette brings this salad together with great flavor.

- 2 (5-oz.) packages sweet baby greens
- 2 Fuji or Honey Crisp apples, halved, cored, and thinly sliced
- Country Ham-Cornbread Croutons
- Muscadine Vinaigrette

1. Divide greens evenly between 12 salad plates. Top evenly with apple slices and Country Ham-Cornbread Croutons. Drizzle with Muscadine Vinaigrette.

Field Greens with Country-Ham Cornbread Croutons and Muscadine Vinaigrette

Country Ham-Cornbread Croutons

Makes about 6 dozen • Hands-On Time: 12 min. • Total Time: 1 hr., 41 min.

- 2   Tbsp. butter
- 1   cup chopped onion
- ½   cup finely chopped country ham
- 2   cups buttermilk
- 1   large egg, lightly beaten
- 1¾ cups plain yellow cornmeal
- 1   tsp. baking powder
- 1   tsp. baking soda
- 1   tsp. salt

1. Preheat oven to 450°. Melt butter in a large skillet over medium-high heat. Add onion and ham. Sauté 6 minutes or until ham is browned and onion is tender. Remove from heat; cool slightly.
2. Combine buttermilk, egg, and sautéed ham mixture in a medium bowl. Combine cornmeal and remaining ingredients in a separate bowl. Gradually add buttermilk mixture to cornmeal mixture, whisking until blended. Pour batter into a lightly greased 13- x 9-inch pan.
3. Bake at 450° for 15 minutes or until golden brown. Cool in pan on a wire rack 10 minutes. Run a knife around edges to loosen cornbread from sides of pan. Remove cornbread from pan; cool completely on a wire rack (about 20 minutes). Reduce oven temperature to 400°.
4. Cut cornbread into 1-inch cubes. Place cornbread cubes in a single layer on a large rimmed baking sheet. Bake at 400° for 18 minutes, stirring occasionally, or until toasted. Cool completely in pan on a wire rack (about 20 minutes).

Muscadine Vinaigrette

Makes 1¼ cups • Hands-On Time: 5 min. • Total Time: 40 min.

- 1¼ cups sweet muscadine wine
- 1   Tbsp. country Dijon mustard
- 1   large shallot, minced
- ½   cup olive oil
- ½   tsp. salt
- ½   tsp. freshly ground pepper

1. Bring wine to a boil over medium-high heat in a small saucepan. Cook 15 minutes or until wine is reduced to ½ cup. Let cool completely (about 20 minutes).
2. Combine wine reduction, mustard, and shallot in a 2-cup glass measuring cup. Gradually add oil in a slow, steady stream, whisking constantly. Whisk in salt and pepper.

Fix It Faster: Instead of making the croutons, use purchased croutons and toss finely chopped country ham into the salad.

Pecan Soup

Makes 13 cups • Hands-On Time: 36 min. • Total Time: 1 hr., 6 min.

This velvety, rich appetizer is like chestnut soup with Southern flair. Ladle it into small cups.

- ½   cup butter
- 3   celery ribs, coarsely chopped
- 2   sweet onions, chopped
- 1   large baking potato, peeled and coarsely chopped
- 4   cups chicken broth
- 3   cups heavy cream
- 1   tsp. salt
- ½   tsp. ground white pepper
- 1   lb. pecan halves, toasted
  Garnishes: crème fraîche, chopped chives, additional pecan halves

1. Melt butter in a Dutch oven over medium heat; add celery and onion. Sauté 20 minutes or until translucent.
2. Add potato and next 5 ingredients. Bring to a boil; reduce heat to medium-low, and simmer, uncovered, 30 minutes or until slightly thickened and potato is very tender. Remove from heat; cool slightly.
3. Process soup mixture, in batches, in a blender until smooth, stopping to scrape down sides as needed. Ladle into serving bowls. Garnish, if desired. Serve hot.

Pecan Soup

Crown Pork Roast with Bourbon-Caramelized Onions and Apples

Makes 12 servings • Hands-On Time: 20 min. • Total Time: 3 hr

Call ahead to your local butcher to reserve this company-worthy roast. Ask the butcher to french the rib bones and tie the roast into a circle with kitchen string for easy roasting.

1 (16-rib) crown pork roast, trimmed and tied (10 to 11 lb.)
1 Tbsp. dried thyme
2 tsp. salt
2 tsp. freshly ground pepper
3 large sweet onions, cut into wedges
1 tsp. salt
1 tsp. freshly ground pepper
2 Braeburn apples, coarsely chopped
2 Tbsp. butter
¼ cup bourbon
Garnishes: fresh thyme sprigs, small lady apples

1. Preheat oven to 450°. Rub meaty portion of ribs with dried thyme, and 2 tsp. each salt and pepper. Place roast in a greased broiler pan. Cap the end of each bone with aluminum foil to prevent tips from burning. Bake at 450° for 20 minutes. Reduce oven temperature to 350°. Bake 2 hours or until a meat thermometer inserted between ribs 2 inches into meat registers 155°. Meanwhile, toss onions with 1 tsp. each salt and pepper. Scatter seasoned onions around pork roast after 1 hour of baking.
2. Carefully transfer roast to a serving platter. Let pork roast stand 15 minutes before slicing. Meanwhile, place broiler pan with onions across 2 burners. Add chopped apple and butter. Cook over medium-high heat 8 minutes or until apples are tender. Remove from heat; stir in bourbon.
3. Spoon onion-apple mixture into middle of roast, if desired. Garnish platter, if desired. To serve, carve roast between bones using a sharp knife.

Note: To keep roast upright, if butcher does not tie crown roast securely into a circle with heavy string, we recommend placing roast, rib ends down, in a 1-qt. round soufflé dish. Place soufflé dish on a baking sheet, and proceed with recipe as directed, except add raw onions to cook with apples in broiler pan, cooking 18 minutes or until onions and apples are tender.

Browned Butter Carrots

Makes 12 servings • Hands-On Time: 23 min. • Total Time: 46 min.

3 lb. carrots
⅓ cup butter
1 tsp. salt
1 tsp. freshly ground pepper
⅓ cup firmly packed dark brown sugar
⅓ cup cider vinegar
2 tsp. vanilla extract
Garnish: fresh herbs such as flat-leaf parsley or thyme

1. Cut carrots in half lengthwise; cut into 2-inch pieces. Cut thick pieces in half lengthwise. Melt butter in an extra-large skillet or sauté pan over medium heat; cook, stirring constantly, 3 minutes or until butter begins to turn golden brown. Add carrots, salt, and pepper; cook 8 to 10 minutes, stirring occasionally, or until carrots are barely tender.
2. Add ½ cup water; cover and cook 10 minutes. Uncover, and add brown sugar and vinegar; cook 8 to 10 minutes or until carrots are glazed and most of liquid evaporates. Remove from heat; stir in vanilla. Garnish, if desired.

White Cheese Grits with Mustard Greens and Bacon

Makes 12 servings • Hands-On Time: 32 min. • Total Time: 32 min.

6 thick bacon slices
5 cups packaged, fresh chopped mustard greens, sliced
Salt and pepper to taste
1 (32-oz.) container chicken broth
2 cups uncooked quick-cooking grits
4 oz. goat cheese, crumbled
⅔ cup whipping cream or half-and-half
2 Tbsp. butter
½ tsp. freshly ground pepper

1. Cook bacon in a skillet over medium heat 8 minutes or until crisp; remove bacon, and drain on paper towels, reserving drippings in skillet. Crumble bacon.
2. Sauté mustard greens in hot drippings 6 to 8 minutes or just until tender. Season with salt and pepper to taste. Set aside.
3. Meanwhile, bring broth and 3 cups water to a boil in a large saucepan over medium-high heat. Gradually whisk in grits; bring to a boil. Reduce heat to medium-low; cover and simmer, stirring occasionally, 5 to 7 minutes or until thickened. Add cheese and remaining 3 ingredients, stirring until cheese and butter are melted. Transfer grits to a serving bowl; spoon sautéed greens down center of grits, and sprinkle with bacon.

Crown Pork Roast with Bourbon-Caramelized
Onions and Apples

White Cheese Grits
with Mustard Greens
and Bacon

Browned Butter Carrots

Caramel-Pear Cake

Makes 12 servings • Hands-On Time: 1 hr. • Total Time: 3 hr., 30 min.

The piece de resistence to any holiday menu should indeed be the dessert. This cake will leave your guests wanting more—because of its cornmeal crumb and yum-factor caramel icing.

HAZELNUT SYRUP

- ½ cup sugar
- 3 Tbsp. hazelnut liqueur

CAKE LAYERS

- 3 cups all-purpose flour
- 1 cup plain yellow cornmeal
- ¾ tsp. salt
- 2 cups butter, softened
- 1½ cups granulated sugar
- 1 cup firmly packed light brown sugar
- 8 large eggs
- ½ cup sour cream
- 1 Tbsp. vanilla extract

CARAMELIZED PEAR FILLING

- ¼ cup butter
- 6 large, firm ripe red D'Anjou or Bartlett pears (2½ lb.), peeled, cored, and chopped
- 2 Tbsp. sugar
- 1 Tbsp. lemon juice
- 1 Tbsp. hazelnut liqueur
- Pinch of salt

CARAMEL FROSTING

- 1½ cups firmly packed light brown sugar
- ¾ cup butter
- 6 Tbsp. evaporated milk or whipping cream
- 2¼ cups powdered sugar
- 1 Tbsp. vanilla extract

1. Prepare Hazelnut Syrup: Combine ¾ cup water and sugar in a small saucepan. Bring to a boil over medium-high heat, stirring frequently. Boil 1 minute or until sugar dissolves. Remove from heat; stir in liqueur. Cool completely; cover and chill thoroughly.

2. Prepare Cake Layers: Preheat oven to 350°. Grease and flour 3 (9-inch) round cake pans; set aside.

3. Combine flour, cornmeal, and salt; set aside. Beat butter at medium speed with a heavy-duty electric mixer until creamy (about 2 minutes). Gradually add sugars, beating well (5 minutes). Add eggs, 1 at a time, beating just until yellow disappears after each addition. Gradually add dry ingredients to butter mixture, beating just until blended after each addition. Stir in sour cream and vanilla. Pour batter into prepared pans.

4. Bake at 350° for 24 to 25 minutes or until a wooden pick inserted in center comes out clean. Cool in pans on a wire rack 10 minutes. Remove from pans to wire rack, and cool completely (about 1 hour).

5. Place each cake layer on a large piece of plastic wrap. Pierce each layer multiple times using a wooden skewer; slowly drizzle or brush Hazelnut Syrup over layers, allowing syrup to soak in. Wrap layers, and refrigerate overnight.

6. Prepare Caramelized Pear Filling: Melt butter in a large skillet or sauté pan over medium-high heat (we had best results with a 12-inch sauté pan). Add pears; sauté 6 minutes or until just tender. Sprinkle pears with sugar and next 3 ingredients. Cook over high heat 6 to 8 minutes or until pears are very tender and beginning to caramelize, stirring twice. Remove from heat; cool to room temperature.

7. Place 1 cake layer on a serving plate; top with half of Caramelized Pear Filling. Top with another cake layer and remaining pear filling. Top with remaining cake layer. Set cake aside while preparing Caramel Frosting.

8. Prepare Caramel Frosting: Bring first 3 ingredients to a boil in a 3-quart saucepan over medium heat, whisking constantly; boil, whisking constantly, 1 minute. Remove from heat; gradually whisk in powdered sugar and vanilla until smooth. Beat vigorously with a wooden spoon 3 to 5 minutes or until mixture begins to cool and thickens slightly. Use immediately.

9. Frost top and sides of cake with Caramel Frosting. Let cake stand at least 1 hour before serving.

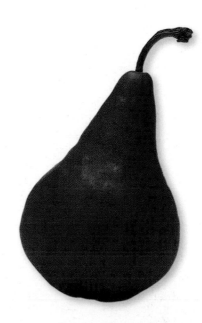

Thanksgiving Family Style,
page 18

Decorate

GET READY TO BE INSPIRED WHETHER
YOU'RE SETTING THE TABLE, WRAPPING
THOUGHTFULLY SELECTED GIFTS, OR
DECKING THE HALLS.

Deck the Halls with FLEA MARKET FINDS

Bring out your lovingly collected things from the kitchen, garage, and attic, and weave them into imaginative displays that say "Merry Christmas" in unexpected ways.

Bowls of Baubles

Don't pass up those yard sale steals or forget those inherited pieces tucked out of sight. Put them to new uses. A tarnished pewter compote or tureen becomes a festive focal point when filled with antique ornaments that show the patina of time. Evergreen boughs tucked in here and there are a simple, natural touch to make this a centerpiece that will last all season. ▼

Pretty as Pie

An inventive arrangement of pie and tart tins and gelatin and brioche molds becomes a glimmering tree of the most unexpected kind. Easy-to-remove Velcro strips keep the assortment secured to a wooden tray that frames the composition. Round out the display with books, accessories, and botanicals in vases—all in complementary hues for interest. ▶

Christmas Cupboard

A rustic red shelf becomes a functional and festive display area for cream china and red and white enamelware pieces. Cherished linens, old tea towels, and embroidered pieces hang from the rod below as a pretty accent. ▲

Vignette of Treasures

White button trees and a garland spool lend a snowy feeling to this silvery display of treasured pieces on the sideboard. Interest comes from layering a bit of the old with the new and the unexpected—silverware, books, and an oversized timepiece framed in grapevine all with ornaments and bows woven in. ▶

Deck the Bar

Reinvent the furniture in your house and put it to new uses this Christmas. Outfit a secretary or china cupboard as a self-service bar with a holiday theme.

Refreshing Decor

Let the party setup become part of your holiday decor. Simple white trays topped with candy, sodas, cocktails, and accessories in repeating hues make a cheerful impression and allow guests to help themselves. ◀ ▲

Visual Impact

Collected blue glassware is a stunner, arranged en masse on cupboard shelves, creating a bright display in the corner of a kitchen. Pops of red from Christmas cards, ornaments, candy canes, and swizzle sticks add interest. ▶

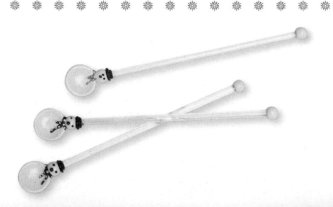

Deck the Sideboard

During this season of gathering together, keep everything you need at your fingertips for easy entertaining and decorating on the fly.

1. Arrange flatware and appetizer plates in a basket to bring to the coffee table in a snap.

2. Keep woody herbs and holly from the winter garden on hand for making arrangements on the fly.

3. Have napkins rolled up and ready for setting the table for impromptu guests.

4. Tuck snips of holly in the spaces between shiny red apples in a bowl for a pretty display.

Merry MANTELS

Perhaps more than any other spot in the house this time of year, this sliver of real estate demands holiday finery.

❋ ❋ ❋ ❋ ❋ ❋ ❋ ❋ ❋ ❋ ❋ ❋ ❋ ❋ ❋ ❋

Turtle Doves

This festive vignette brings the outdoors in with birds, branches, and boughs placed by the chimney with care. The interesting form of winged elm twigs in bell jars filled with faux snow will last indefinitely. Artificial snowballs and a dusting of more snow carry the wintery look across the mantelpiece, providing a bit of shimmer in the candlelight. A coordinating palette of green, blue, gold and bronze provides a cohesive look. Objects and a collection of bird figurines are placed at varying heights, using vintage clothbound books as risers, to add interest. Stockings filled with tiny wrapped packages repeat the cool hues and bird theme.

❋ ❋ ❋ ❋ ❋ ❋ ❋ ❋ ❋ ❋ ❋ ❋ ❋ ❋ ❋ ❋

✳ ✳ ✳ ✳ ✳ ✳ ✳ ✳ ✳ ✳ ✳

Wire, welded into three-dimensional shapes, is fastened into a modern garland that is a striking accent against the bleached surround. ▲

The shimmer of firelight bounces off the marble surround reflecting onto the abstract painting above. Greenery from the garden is embellished with silver paint and tucked around and between an assortment of candles and shimmery ornaments. ◀

✳ ✳ ✳ ✳ ✳ ✳ ✳ ✳ ✳ ✳ ✳

Botanical Beauty

Weeping pine boughs with their diminutive cones add a lacy, feminine quality to this design. A fitting accent to the angelic artwork and fragrant paperwhites. ▼

Merry Mix

An assortment of candlesticks of varying styles and materials works together to form a charming vignette. ►

Festive FLOWERS

With a Christmas palette to inspire you, think beyond poinsettias and holly and turn to less commonly used blooms that shout, "Be merry!"

❋ ❋

Modern Mix

A grouping of white vases is striking with an assortment of vibrant blooms bursting forth. Blushing tulips continue to grow once cut and their weeping habit adds interest to the upright stance of crimson peonies and lacy hydrangeas. The organic shapes and textures of the vases are an ideal canvas for the oranges, clementines, kumquats, and pomegranates, which continue the complementary hues. Metallic sphere ornaments repeat the circular shapes of the fruit.

❋ ❋

❀ ❀ ❀ ❀ ❀ ❀ ❀ ❀ ❀ ❀ ❀ ❀ ❀ ❀ ❀

High Wire Act

Single stems strikingly arranged can lend loads of drama. Stand-alone tulip stems are nestled into test tube-size inserts set into a series of wire holders. Lacy greenery and hypericum berries are added randomly for interest. ▲ ▶

❀ ❀ ❀ ❀ ❀ ❀ ❀ ❀ ❀ ❀ ❀ ❀ ❀ ❀ ❀

❀ ❀ ❀ ❀ ❀ ❀ ❀ ❀ ❀ ❀ ❀ ❀ ❀ ❀ ❀

Jolly Greeting

On a chest in this home's foyer, guests are greeted with a cheery display of gerbera daisies and berry-covered branches tucked into a contemporary wire filigree box. Pearlized ornaments underscore the Christmas theme. ◀

❀ ❀ ❀ ❀ ❀ ❀ ❀ ❀ ❀ ❀ ❀ ❀ ❀ ❀ ❀

Cup o' Cheer

Mugs with painted stars and curvaceous numerals count down the days until Christmas. Filled with a mix of holiday goodies and pretty botanicals, this seemingly haphazard arrangement of stacked and overlapping cups serves as eye candy on mantel or windowsill to be enjoyed throughout the season. Chartreuse mums are a vibrant pairing with red berries and the silvery-flocked wreath above. Look for treats in similar colors to lend impact when they peer over the rim.

❉ ❉ ❉ ❉ ❉ ❉ ❉ ❉ ❉ ❉ ❉ ❉ ❉ ❉ ❉ ❉ ❉ ❉ ❉

Traditional with a Twist

Mercury glass votives and metallic trees shimmer against a sub-
dued backdrop of wood paneling and an antique tapestry. A heavy
wrought-iron vessel filled with floral foam anchors this display of
ruffly scarlet amaryllis. Evergreen boughs are tucked in for texture
and spill out on the old rectory table. An abundant spray of ilex
berries and architectural twisting willow branches draw the eye
upward, adding drama to this stunning centerpiece.

❉ ❉ ❉ ❉ ❉ ❉ ❉ ❉ ❉ ❉ ❉ ❉ ❉ ❉ ❉ ❉ ❉ ❉

Inspired PLACE SETTINGS

White bone china is both practical and versatile. It's the perfect canvas for elegant food and is to a table setting what a little black dress is to a hostess.

❋ ❋ ❋ ❋ ❋ ❋ ❋ ❋ ❋ ❋ ❋ ❋ ❋ ❋

Glamorous Glimmer

The fire is roaring, Christmas carols are playing, guests are arriving, and the aroma of the holiday feast wafts through the air. The glimmer of gold ribbon and ornaments reflect the fire and candlelight while the shimmer of beaded red place mats draw the eye to the gathering place for the meal to come. Rimmed cream soup bowls and saucers rest on simple white plates and suggest the multicourse meal ahead. The overall effect is one of timeless, Old World grace, certain to leave an imprint in memory.

❋ ❋ ❋ ❋ ❋ ❋ ❋ ❋ ❋ ❋ ❋ ❋ ❋ ❋

❋ ❋ ❋ ❋ ❋ ❋ ❋ ❋ ❋ ❋ ❋ ❋ ❋ ❋

1. A white dinner plate sets off a salad plate rimmed in a silvery fish scale pattern and a circular silver mat beneath, lending a touch of Hollywood glamour to this table.

2. Vintage celadon and gold china framed by crisp white looks fresh and new. Ornaments, boxwood wreaths, and tinted glassware complete the look.

3. This setting is as much traditional Christmas as mod masterpiece. Red and white are taken to new heights with a mix of pattern and stripes divided by a band of white.

4. Minimalist becomes masterful in this juxtaposition of circle and square, gold and snow white. Translucent ornaments and whitewashed turtledove votives add just enough interest.

❋ ❋ ❋ ❋ ❋ ❋ ❋ ❋ ❋ ❋ ❋ ❋ ❋ ❋

Rustic wicker chargers and engraved pewter silverware are a perfect pairing with whimsical china accented with painted Christmas scenes from a bygone era. The red and green tartan plaid is equally retro and all the pieces work beautifully together to create a jolly table that isn't the least bit stuffy. These are the plates to be passed down for generations and remembered fondly from childhood—the ones to load up with cookies for Santa and put away carefully until next year.

Twelve Ways at CHRISTMAS

From the dozens of greeting cards and numerous gifts to wrap to doors to embellish for the season, we've got a dozen inspired ideas to take the ho-hum out of your annual displays.

3 WAYS WITH GREETING CARDS

✹ ✹ ✹ ✹ ✹ ✹ ✹ ✹ ✹ ✹ ✹ ✹ ✹ ✹ ✹

1. A tree fabricated from industrial rebar becomes a miniature tree of treasured greetings to enjoy and share.
2. Grapevine wrapped around a galvanized spire is a modern twist on the tree. Wire snowflake accents are ideal for holding favorite cards.
3. A cast-off piece of fabricated metalwork becomes a colorful indoor wreath-cardholder for the door.

✹ ✹ ✹ ✹ ✹ ✹ ✹ ✹ ✹ ✹ ✹ ✹ ✹ ✹ ✹

3 WAYS WITH GIFT WRAP

1. Ornamental Touches

Last year's ornaments, tinsel and garland can easily be turned into this year's inventive packaging. Miniature wreaths which originated as napkin rings find new life in place of the usual bows. Birch boxes and ornaments are gussied up with paint to become pretty containers and toppers for presents. Foam snowflakes and a jingle bell garland are an elegant pairing atop simple silver foil wrapping paper.

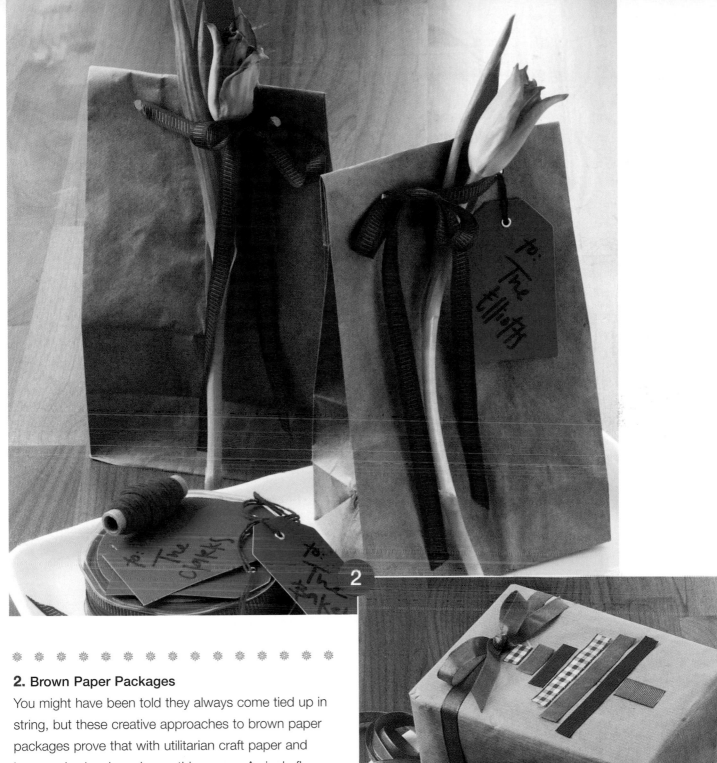

2. Brown Paper Packages

You might have been told they always come tied up in string, but these creative approaches to brown paper packages prove that with utilitarian craft paper and inexpensive lunch sacks anything goes. A single flower stem, ribbon and gift tag turn a plain goodie back into something spectacular. Scrap ribbon can be used in novel ways too, as in the one-dimensional tree glued to the woodsy brown backdrop below. Simply center graduating lengths of ribbon and finish with a bow topper and a tiny trunk.

3

3. Uncommon Objects

Look beyond the gift-wrap closet and craft store for interesting ideas to decorate gifts for friends and family. Castoffs from a child's dressup trunk or your closet can be repurposed in inventive ways such as these belted beauties. The kitchen or garden shed are sure to hold unusual but fitting items for topping a gift for the cook (like these disposable bamboo spoons) or the loved one with a green thumb. Let your imagination run wild.

6 SIMPLY DAZZLING DOORS

❄ ❄ ❄ ❄ ❄ ❄ ❄ ❄ ❄ ❄ ❄ ❄ ❄ ❄ ❄ ❄

1. Super simple but simply stunning, a storebought wreath is further embellished with reindeer moss and berries and tied with an iridescent bow to complement the red door.

2. This monochromatic masterpiece is a study in silver. Forget the messy flocking, a generous misting of spray paint does the trick and the result is magical.

3. Against a white backdrop, Christmas red and green comes to life. Ibex berry branches are woven into a loosely formed wreath that will last for weeks.

4. The russett red of this dense circle of pepperberries is a pretty tone-on-tone approach to this stately front door or richly-stained wood.

❄ ❄ ❄ ❄ ❄ ❄ ❄ ❄ ❄ ❄ ❄ ❄ ❄ ❄ ❄ ❄

5. A dose of vintage whimsy brings this porch to jolly life. A wood and tin Santa greets all who enter while his sled stands at the ready when it's time to hit the North Pole. Red satin bows draw the eye upward while miniature pine trees are mulched with ruby ornaments with a gleaming satin finish.

6. The side entry isn't forgotten. A mass of evergreen boughs of varying types are wired to a metal tree-shaped frame that can be used year after year.

Deck the Halls with Flea Market Finds, page 52

Savor

FROM OUR TEST KITCHENS TO
YOUR HOME KITCHEN, THIS YEAR'S
ASSORTMENT OF RECIPES OFFERS
UP IDEAS FOR BREAKFAST THROUGH
DESSERT AND EVERY COURSE IN
BETWEEN. THESE INSPIRED DISHES
ARE SURE TO BECOME YEAR-ROUND
FAVORITES.

Five O'clock SOMEWHERE

Raise a glass and spread some cheer, Christmastime is almost here.
Savor it with these spirited cocktails and light nibbles.

 *quick & easy*

Ginger-Cranberry Mojito

Makes 1 serving • Hands-On Time: 6 min. • Total Time: 6 min.

Ginger beer is basically ginger ale with a much stronger ginger flavor. It's available in alcoholic and nonalcoholic versions. The beer adds the expected Mojito fizz, while cranberry juice adds a splash of color.

- ¼ cup lightly packed torn fresh mint leaves
- 1 Tbsp. superfine sugar
- ½ lime, cut into fourths
- Crushed ice
- ½ cup cranberry juice cocktail
- ½ cup ginger beer
- ¼ cup light rum
- Garnishes: fresh mint sprigs, skewered cranberries

1. Place first 3 ingredients in 1 (12-oz.) glass; muddle (crush together) until sugar dissolves. Fill glass with ice, filling three-fourths full. Add cranberry juice, ginger beer, and rum; stir. Garnish, if desired. Serve immediately.

 *quick & easy*

Celebration Champagne Punch

Makes 8 cups • Hands-On Time: 5 min. • Total Time: 5 min.

We liked this bracer just as well without the schnapps.

- ¼ cup orange liqueur
- ¼ cup cinnamon schnapps
- ½ tsp. aromatic bitters
- ¼ tsp. freshly grated nutmeg
- 1 (20-oz.) can pineapple tidbits, undrained
- 1 orange, thinly sliced
- 1 (750-milliliter) bottle extra dry Champagne or sparkling wine, chilled
- Ice

1. Stir together first 6 ingredients in a punch bowl or large pitcher. Gently stir in Champagne just before serving.

 *quick & easy*

Apple Tea Punch

Makes 12 cups • Hands-On Time: 5 min. • Total Time: 5 min.

Sweet tea vodka makes this punch unique.

- 2 (750-milliliter) bottles sparkling water, chilled
- 1 (750-milliliter) bottle sweet tea-flavored vodka, chilled
- 1 (12-oz.) can frozen apple juice concentrate, thawed
- 1 (10-oz.) jar whole red maraschino cherries (with stems), drained
- 2 lemons, thinly sliced
- 1 Gala apple, unpeeled and thinly sliced crosswise
- Ice

1. Combine first 4 ingredients in a punch bowl. Add lemon and apple slices. Serve immediately over ice.

Celebration Champagne Punch

Apple Tea Punch

Ginger-Cranberry
Mojito

Ginger-Pear Sparkle,
page 96

 *editor's favorite ~ quick & easy*

Ginger-Pear Sparkle

(pictured on page 95)

Makes 8½ cups • Hands-On Time: 4 min. • Total Time: 8 min.

Pear nectar gives body and pure pear flavor to this drink. It can be found canned or bottled on the soda aisle.

- 4 cups ginger ale
- 2 cups pear nectar
- 2 cups pear-flavored vodka
- ½ cup Ginger Simple Syrup
- 2 Tbsp. fresh lemon juice
  Ice cubes
  Garnish: pear slices

1. Combine first 5 ingredients in a pitcher. Serve over ice. Garnish, if desired.

Ginger Simple Syrup

Makes 1 cup • Hands-On Time: 2 min. • Total Time: 4 min.

- 1 cup sugar
- 1 (3-inch) piece fresh ginger, thinly sliced

1. Microwave sugar, ginger, and ½ cup water in a 2-cup glass measuring cup at HIGH 1 minute; stir. Microwave at HIGH 1 more minute or until sugar is dissolved. Remove and discard ginger. Cover and chill syrup until ready to use.

quick & easy

Kentucky's Mark

Makes 2 servings • Hands-On Time: 3 min. • Total Time: 3 min.

Honey and a touch of spice complement the natural flavor of bourbon in this strong sipper meant for a holiday celebration.

- ⅓ cup bourbon
- 1 Tbsp. honey
- ½ tsp. aromatic bitters
  Crushed ice
- ¼ cup ginger ale
  Garnish: orange zest curls

1. Combine first 4 ingredients in a cocktail shaker or martini shaker. Cover with lid, and shake vigorously until thoroughly chilled (about 20 seconds). Remove lid, and strain into 2 glasses with ice. Pour 2 Tbsp. ginger ale into each glass. Garnish, if desired. Serve immediately.

A red straw tray atop a table becomes the ideal bar setup with everything at the ready—muddlers, drink stirs, a cocktail shaker and the evening's elixirs. ▼

Kentucky's Mark

Lemon Basil Martinis

Poinsettia Sangría

editor's favorite ~ make ahead

Lemon Basil Martinis

Makes 7 servings • Hands-On Time: 19 min. • Total Time: 1 hr., 19 min.

A homemade herb-infused sweet-and-sour mix is the key to this refreshing cocktail. Unused sweet-and-sour mix can be stored in the refrigerator for up to one month. Use it to make margaritas or other cocktails calling for sweet-and-sour mix.

1¼ cups superfine sugar
¾   cup loosely packed fresh lemon basil leaves, torn
    into pieces*
1¼ cups fresh lemon juice
¼   cup fresh lime juice
1¾ cups vodka
    Crushed ice
    Garnishes: lemon zest curls

1. Bring sugar and 1 cup water to a boil in a medium sauce-pan over medium-high heat. Boil, stirring often, 1 minute or until sugar is dissolved and mixture is clear. Remove from heat; add torn basil, and cool completely (about 1 hour). Remove and discard basil. Stir in juices; pour into a pitcher or glass jar. Cover and chill thoroughly.
2. For each martini, combine ½ cup chilled sweet-and-sour syrup mixture and ¼ cup vodka in a cocktail shaker; fill with crushed ice. Cover with lid, and shake vigorously until thoroughly chilled (about 30 seconds).
3. Strain into a chilled martini glass. Garnish, if desired.

*Regular fresh basil leaves may be substituted.

quick & easy

Poinsettia Sangría

Makes 6½ cups • Hands-On Time: 6 min. • Total Time: 6 min.

Deep red like a Christmas poinsettia, this Spanish punch displays a ruby-colored theme beautifully.

1   (750-milliliter) bottle dry red wine
1   cup sliced strawberries
¼   cup orange liqueur
¼   cup thawed frozen cranberry juice cocktail
1   Gala apple, unpeeled and thinly sliced
1   pt. fresh raspberries
    Garnishes: Garnishes: sliced strawberries, sliced apple,
    fresh raspberries

1. Combine all ingredients in a large pitcher. Cover and chill 1 to 8 hours. Garnish, if desired.

Country Ham Rolls with Orange Mustard

Makes 16 servings • Hands-On Time: 19 min. • Total Time: 41 min.

These meaty rolls make a great choice for a brunch buffet line.

- 1 (11-oz.) package Parker House-style frozen yeast rolls, thawed
- 2 Tbsp. butter, melted
- 1 (8-oz.) package thin-sliced country ham
- ½ cup orange marmalade
- 2 Tbsp. Dijon mustard
- 2 Tbsp. brown sugar

1. Brush tops of rolls with melted butter. Heat rolls according to package directions.

2. Meanwhile, brown country ham slices in a large skillet over medium-high heat 1 to 2 minutes on each side. Remove from heat, reserving drippings in skillet. Cut ham into serving-size pieces; cover and keep warm.

3. Combine marmalade, mustard, and brown sugar in skillet; cook 1 to 2 minutes or until melted and smooth. Remove from heat.

4. Split rolls, and spread evenly with orange-mustard mixture. Stuff rolls with ham. Serve warm or at room temperature.

Ham-Wrapped Olive Shrimp

Makes 30 appetizer servings • Hands-On Time: 17 min. • Total Time: 53 min.

¼ cup olive oil
1½ tsp. lemon zest
3 Tbsp. fresh lemon juice
¾ tsp. dried crushed red pepper
¼ tsp. salt
30 large peeled, raw shrimp (about 1 lb.)
10 very thin deli ham slices
30 pimiento-stuffed Spanish olives

1. Whisk together oil, lemon zest, juice, red pepper, and salt in a large bowl. Add shrimp; toss to coat. Cover and chill 30 minutes.
2. Preheat broiler with oven rack 5½ inches from heat. Cut each ham slice into 3 lengthwise strips. Wrap each strip of ham around 1 shrimp and 1 olive; secure with a wooden pick. Place wrapped shrimp on a large lightly greased baking sheet. Repeat procedure with remaining ham, shrimp, and olives.
3. Broil 3 minutes on each side or until shrimp turn pink. Arrange appetizers on a serving platter. Serve hot.

Mini Herbed Frittatas with Smoked Salmon and Crème Fraîche

Makes 2 dozen • Hands-On Time: 11 min. • Total Time: 37 min.

1 Tbsp. butter
½ cup finely chopped red onion
8 large eggs, lightly beaten
½ cup (2 oz.) shredded Havarti cheese
1 Tbsp. chopped fresh dill
¼ tsp. salt
¼ tsp. freshly ground pepper
3 oz. smoked salmon, coarsely chopped
¼ cup crème fraîche
Garnishes: fresh dill sprigs, caviar

1. Preheat oven to 350°.
2. Melt butter in a medium skillet over medium-high heat. Add onion; sauté 2 minutes or until tender.
3. Combine sautéed onion and next 5 ingredients in a medium bowl; stir well. Pour egg mixture evenly into 2 well-greased (12-cup) miniature muffin pans, filling full.
4. Bake at 350° for 20 minutes or until egg mixture is set. Cool in pans on a wire rack 3 to 4 minutes; remove from pans. Top each frittata with salmon and ½ tsp. crème fraîche. Garnish, if desired.

Ham-Wrapped Olive Shrimp

Mini Herbed Frittatas With Smoked Salmon and Crème Fraîche

quick & easy

Italian Nachos

Makes 8 to 10 appetizer servings • Hands-On Time: 4 min. • Total Time: 28 min.

An Italian flavor spin is a delicious fit for this quintessential pickup food. Substitute mozzarella for the cheese blend, if desired.

- 1 (13-oz.) package tortilla chips
- 1 lb. mild Italian sausage, casings removed
- ½ cup chopped red onion
- 3 garlic cloves, minced
- 2 Tbsp. butter
- 2 Tbsp. all-purpose flour
- 2 cups milk
- ¾ cup (3 oz.) grated Asiago cheese
- 1 cup pepperoncini salad pepper rings, drained
- ½ cup pitted kalamata olives, chopped
- ¼ tsp. dried crushed red pepper
- 1 (12-oz.) jar roasted red bell peppers, drained and coarsely chopped
- 1 (12-oz.) jar marinated quartered artichoke hearts, drained and chopped
- 3 cups (12 oz.) shredded Italian six-cheese blend

1. Preheat oven to 400°. Scatter two-thirds of chips onto a parchment paper-lined large rimmed baking sheet. Set aside. (Reserve remaining chips for other uses.)
2. Brown sausage in a large skillet over medium-high heat, stirring often, 6 to 8 minutes or until meat crumbles and is no longer pink; drain. Remove from skillet, reserving drippings in skillet. Set aside sausage. Sauté red onion and garlic in drippings over medium-high heat 2 to 3 minutes or until tender. Set aside.
3. Melt butter in a heavy saucepan over low heat; whisk in flour until smooth. Cook 1 minute, whisking constantly. Gradually whisk in milk; cook over medium heat, whisking constantly, until mixture is thickened and bubbly. Remove from heat; stir in Asiago cheese until melted.
4. Drizzle cheese sauce over chips; top with reserved sausage and sautéed onion mixture. Top with pepperoncini, olives, crushed red pepper, roasted peppers, and artichoke hearts. Sprinkle with 3 cups cheese blend.
5. Bake at 400° for 4 to 5 minutes or until cheese is melted. Gently remove nachos with parchment paper onto a serving platter, if desired. Serve hot.

Pizza Cups

make ahead

Pizza Cups

Makes 32 appetizer servings • Hands-On Time: 32 min. • Total Time: 44 min.

Make ahead and freeze these bite-size appetizers suitable for all ages. You'll need several mini muffin pans here—they're inexpensive to collect.

- ¼ (1-lb.) package mild ground pork sausage
- ⅓ cup finely chopped green bell pepper
- ½ cup (1.5 oz.) pepperoni slices, chopped (about 20)
- 6 pimiento-stuffed Spanish olives, chopped
- 1 cup (4 oz.) shredded Italian six-cheese blend
- ¾ cup freshly grated Parmesan cheese
- 1 (16.3-oz.) can refrigerated flaky biscuits
- ½ cup pizza sauce
- Freshly ground pepper

1. Preheat oven to 400°. Brown sausage in a small skillet over medium-high heat, stirring often, until meat crumbles and is no longer pink; drain. Sauté bell pepper 1 to 2 minutes or just until tender. Combine sausage, bell pepper, pepperoni, and olives.
2. Combine cheeses. Cut each biscuit into fourths; roll each biscuit piece into a ball. Roll each ball into a 3-inch circle using a lightly floured rolling pin. Press rounds into cups of 3 lightly greased (12-cup) miniature muffin pans. (Dough will come up sides, forming a cup.)

3. Spoon sausage mixture evenly into cups. Top evenly with pizza sauce. Sprinkle evenly with cheese and freshly ground pepper.

4. Bake at 400° for 11 to 12 minutes or until golden. Serve hot.

Note: To reheat frozen Pizza Cups, thaw desired amount in refrigerator overnight. Place on a baking sheet. Bake at 350° for 10 minutes.

 make ahead

Spicy Pumpkin Hummus on Green Onion Griddle Cakes

Makes 11 servings (about 22 cakes) • Hands-On Time: 26 min. • Total Time: 34 min.

For a fun presentation, stack these small savory cakes for each serving. Spread any leftover pumpkin hummus on sandwiches, or spoon it into jars and give as gifts.

SPICY PUMPKIN HUMMUS
    3   garlic cloves, halved
    1   (16-oz.) can chickpeas, drained
    3   Tbsp. extra virgin olive oil
    1   cup canned pumpkin
    ½   cup freshly grated Parmesan cheese
    2   Tbsp. fresh lemon juice
    2   tsp. minced canned chipotle pepper in adobo sauce
    ½   tsp. salt

GREEN ONION GRIDDLE CAKES
    1¼   cups all-purpose baking mix
    ¾   cup milk
    ⅓   cup chopped green onions
    ¼   cup Greek yogurt
    ¼   tsp. salt
    1   Tbsp. butter, melted
    Garnish: thinly sliced green onions

1. Prepare Spicy Pumpkin Hummus: Pulse garlic in a food processor 4 or 5 times or until minced. Add chickpeas, and process 20 seconds or until smooth, stopping to scrape down sides as needed. With processor running, pour oil through food chute; scrape down sides as needed. Add pumpkin and next 4 ingredients; pulse 5 or 6 times or just until blended. Cover and chill until ready to serve.

2. Prepare Green Onion Griddle Cakes: Combine baking mix and next 4 ingredients in a medium bowl, stirring just until blended (do not overmix).

3. Pour about 1 Tbsp. batter for each griddle cake onto a hot, lightly buttered griddle or large nonstick skillet over medium heat. Cook griddle cakes 2 to 3 minutes or until tops are covered with bubbles and edges look dry and cooked; turn and cook 1 to 2 more minutes.

4. For each serving, stack 2 griddle cakes, If desired, and spoon 1½ Tbsp. hummus onto stack. Garnish, if desired.

Spicy Pumpkin Hummus on Green Onion Griddle Cakes

Fig-Glazed Ham

Main ATTRACTIONS

Inspired and fabulous, these foolproof entrées will
make a lasting impression.

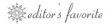 *editor's favorite*

Fig-Glazed Ham

Makes 10 to 12 servings • Hands-On Time: 10 min. • Total Time: 1 hr., 40 min.

This ham is a knockout of a dish, thanks to an amazing glaze.

- 1 (10- to 12-lb.) fully cooked, bone-in ham
- 1 red onion, vertically sliced
- 4 red pears, cored and cut into fourths
- 1 (11.5-oz.) jar fig preserves
- ½ cup Madeira
- ⅓ cup honey
- 3 Tbsp. aged balsamic vinegar
- 1 Tbsp. chopped crystallized ginger
- 1 Tbsp. chopped fresh rosemary
  Garnishes: fresh rosemary sprigs

1. Preheat oven to 350°. Remove skin from ham; trim fat to ¼-inch thickness. Make shallow cuts in fat 1 inch apart in a diamond pattern. Place ham in a lightly greased roasting pan. Arrange onion and pears around ham in pan.
2. Stir together fig preserves and next 5 ingredients; spoon 1 cup preserves mixture over ham. Insert a meat thermometer into ham, making sure it does not touch fat or bone.
3. Bake at 350° on lowest oven rack 1½ to 2 hours or until thermometer registers 140°, basting with remaining preserves mixture and pan juices every 30 minutes. (Cover ham with aluminum foil after 1 hour, if necessary, to prevent excessive browning.)
4. Transfer ham to a serving platter. Remove pears from pan with a slotted spoon; arrange around ham on platter. Garnish platter, if desired.
5. Meanwhile, transfer pan drippings with ham to a saucepan; simmer 3 minutes over medium heat. Spoon desired amount of pan drippings over ham and pears. Serve remaining drippings as a sauce.

Steak au Poivre with Cognac Mushrooms

Makes 4 servings • Hands-On Time: 23 min. • Total Time: 35 min.

Here's an easy yet impressive entrée that puts the Southern black cast-iron skillet to its best use.

- 4 (6- to 8-oz.) beef tenderloin fillets (2 inches thick)
- 1 Tbsp. olive oil
- 3 Tbsp. mixed peppercorns, crushed
- ½ tsp. salt, divided
- ¼ cup butter, divided
- 1 shallot, minced
- 1 (8-oz.) package sliced fresh mushrooms
- ¼ cup cognac
- ¼ cup beef broth
- ½ cup heavy cream
  Garnish: fresh flat-leaf parsley

1. Preheat oven to 425°. Rub fillets with olive oil; sprinkle with crushed peppercorns and ¼ tsp. salt, pressing to adhere.
2. Melt 2 Tbsp. butter in a cast-iron skillet over medium-high heat. Add fillets to pan; cook 2 to 3 minutes on each side or until browned. Place skillet in oven. Bake at 425° for 12 minutes or until desired degree of doneness. Remove fillets from skillet; transfer to a serving platter, and keep warm.
3. Melt remaining 2 Tbsp. butter in cast-iron skillet over medium-high heat. Add shallot and mushrooms; sauté 10 minutes or until tender. Add cognac and broth. Cook 5 minutes or until liquid is reduced by half. Stir in heavy cream and remaining ¼ tsp. salt. Cook 5 minutes or until sauce is thickened. Spoon sauce over fillets. Garnish, if desired.

Cajun-Stuffed Pork Roast

Cajun-Stuffed Pork Roast

Makes 10 to 12 servings • Hands-On Time: 1 hr., 2 min. • Total Time: 2 hr., 5 min., including cream

- ½ lb. peeled, small raw shrimp, chopped
- 1 red bell pepper, chopped
- 1 green bell pepper, chopped
- 3 Tbsp. Cajun seasoning, divided
- 1 (3½-lb.) boneless pork loin
- ¼ cup butter, softened
- Andouille Cream

1. Preheat oven to 450°. Toss together shrimp, peppers, and 1 Tbsp. Cajun seasoning. Place mixture on a lightly greased baking sheet. Bake at 450° for 15 minutes or until shrimp turn pink and peppers start to caramelize. Let cool 10 minutes.

2. Meanwhile, trim pork loin roast. Butterfly pork loin by making a horizontal cut (about one-third down from top) into 1 side of pork, cutting to within ½ inch of other side. (Do not cut all the way through roast.)

3. Unfold top cut piece, open, and lay flat. Butterfly and repeat procedure on opposite side of remaining two-thirds portion of pork loin, beginning at top or bottom of inside cut.

4. Place pork between 2 sheets of heavy-duty plastic wrap, and flatten to ½-inch thickness, using a rolling pin or flat side of a meat mallet. Spread 2 Tbsp. butter over pork; sprinkle with 1 Tbsp. Cajun seasoning. Spread shrimp mixture over pork, leaving a ½-inch border. Roll up, starting at 1 long side, and tie with kitchen string, securing at 2-inch intervals. Rub remaining 2 Tbsp. butter over roast; season with remaining 1 Tbsp. Cajun seasoning. Place roast on a lightly greased rack in a roasting pan.

5. Bake at 450° for 20 minutes. Reduce oven temperature to 325°, and bake 1 hour or until a meat thermometer inserted into thickest portion registers 155°. Cover with aluminum foil, and let rest 20 minutes. Slice pork into 1-inch pieces; serve with Andouille Cream.

Andouille Cream

Makes 3 cups • Hands-On Time: 31 min. • Total Time: 35 min.

- ½ lb. andouille sausage, chopped
- 4 cups heavy cream
- 1 Tbsp. Creole mustard

1. Cook sausage in a large skillet over medium-high heat, stirring often, 5 to 6 minutes or until browned.

2. Add cream; cook over medium heat for 30 minutes, stirring occasionally, or until cream is thickened and reduced by half. Stir in mustard. Remove from heat.

Roasted Veal Chops with Mushrooms and Vermouth

Makes 4 servings • Hands-On Time: 32 min. • Total Time: 1 hr., 27 min.

- 2 Tbsp. chopped fresh oregano
- 2 Tbsp. chopped flat-leaf parsley
- 2 Tbsp. chopped fresh thyme
- 2 tsp. lemon zest
- 1 tsp. kosher salt
- 1 tsp. freshly ground pepper
- 2 garlic cloves, finely chopped
- 4 (12- to 14-oz.) veal rib chops (about 1¼ inches thick)
- 2 Tbsp. olive oil
- 1 Tbsp. butter
- 1 (14-oz.) can quartered artichoke hearts, drained
- 1 (8-oz.) package baby portobello mushrooms, halved
- 4 garlic cloves
- 2 large shallots, thinly sliced
- 1 cup dry vermouth
- ½ cup chicken broth
- 2 Tbsp. fresh lemon juice
- ¼ cup butter, cut into pieces
- 1 cup instant polenta
- Garnish: fresh herb sprigs

1. Combine first 7 ingredients; rub evenly over veal chops. Let chops stand 30 minutes.

2. Preheat oven to 400°. Heat oil and 1 Tbsp. butter in a large skillet over medium-high heat until butter melts. Add veal chops; cook 2 to 3 minutes on each side or until browned. Remove veal from skillet; place in a shallow roasting pan. Arrange artichoke hearts, mushrooms, 4 garlic cloves, and shallots around chops. Bake at 400° for 25 minutes or until a meat thermometer inserted into thickest portion of veal registers 160°.

3. Transfer chops, artichokes, and mushrooms from roasting pan to a serving platter; pour any accumulated pan juices and browned bits into large skillet. Add vermouth, broth, and lemon juice. Bring to a boil over medium-high heat; boil 10 minutes or until reduced by half. Reduce heat to low; add ¼ cup butter, 1 Tbsp. at a time, stirring until butter melts and sauce is slightly thickened.

4. Meanwhile, cook polenta according to package directions. Serve chops with hot cooked polenta and vermouth pan sauce. Garnish, if desired.

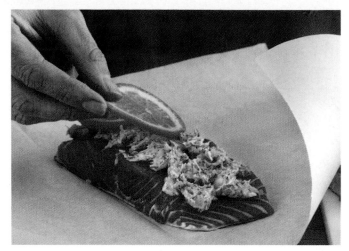

Place salmon next to fold of parchment paper, and top with Dill-Shallot Butter and lemon slices.

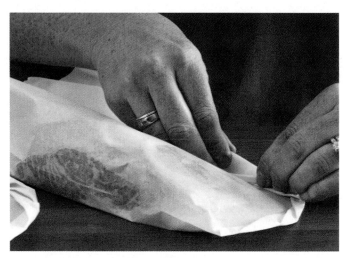

Fold paper over salmon, and seal by crimping the edges with small folds. Bake as directed.

Carefully open packets, and garnish with a fresh dill sprig to serve.

Wild Salmon Parcels with Dill-Shallot Butter

Makes 12 servings • Hands-On Time: 15 min. • Total Time: 38 min.

Ask your fishmonger to remove the scales and pin bones from the salmon fillets. To remove the bones yourself, run your finger along the length of the fillet to expose the pin bones. Pull them out one at a time with needle-nose pliers or small tongs.

12 (8-oz.) wild salmon fillets (1 inch thick)
　Parchment paper
1 Tbsp. kosher salt
1 Tbsp. freshly ground pepper
　Dill-Shallot Butter, softened
18 thin lemon slices, halved
　Garnishes: dill sprigs, lemon wedges

1. Preheat oven to 375°. Cut 12 (15 x 10-inch) pieces of parchment paper. Fold each paper in half crosswise and crease, then open each. Place 1 fillet near fold of each piece. Sprinkle fish with salt and pepper, and spread with Dill-Shallot Butter. Top with lemon slices. Fold paper; seal edges well with narrow folds. Place packets on 2 large baking sheets.
2. Bake at 375° for 12 minutes, placing 1 pan on middle oven rack and another on lower oven rack. Switch pans, and bake 11 more minutes or until desired degree of doneness. Garnish, if desired. Serve immediately.

Dill-Shallot Butter

Makes 1⅓ cups • Hands-On Time: 11 min. • Total Time: 11 min.

1 cup European-style unsalted butter*, softened
¼ cup finely chopped fresh dill
2 Tbsp. lemon zest
1 tsp. kosher salt
½ tsp. freshly ground pepper
3 shallots, minced

1. Place all ingredients in a medium bowl. Beat at medium speed with an electric mixer until blended. Store in an airtight container up to 1 week, or freeze up to 1 month.

*European-style butter is cultured butter made from cream that has been both pasteurized and fermented yielding a more aromatic and buttery-flavor. Regular unsalted butter may be substituted.

Maple-Brined Turkey Breast with Currant-Stuffed Baked Apples

Makes 12 servings • Hands-On Time: 15 min. • Total Time: 3 hr., 56 min., including apples plus 1 day for chilling

- 1 cup firmly packed dark brown sugar
- ½ cup maple syrup
- ¼ cup salt
- ¼ cup soy sauce
- 2 tsp. peppercorns
- 4 bay leaves
- 3 (3-inch) cinnamon sticks
- 1 (6- to 7-lb.) skin-on, bone-in turkey breast
- 1 small onion, quartered
- 1 small Braeburn apple, cored and quartered
- ¼ cup fresh thyme sprigs
- ½ lemon, cut into 3 pieces
- 2 Tbsp. olive oil
- 2 Tbsp. butter, melted
- ½ cup maple syrup
- ¼ cup frozen apple juice concentrate, thawed
- Currant-Stuffed Baked Apples
- Garnishes: fresh sage, orange wedges, cranberries, apples

1. Combine first 7 ingredients and 1 qt. water in a Dutch oven; bring to a boil over medium heat, stirring until sugar and salt dissolve. Remove from heat; stir in 1 more qt. water. Let cool completely.

2. Place turkey, breast side down, in 2-gal. food-safe container. Gradually add brine. Cover and chill 8 hours or overnight, turning at least twice.

3. Remove turkey from brine; discard brine. Rinse turkey, and pat dry with paper towels.

4. Preheat oven to 325°. Place onion, apple, ¼ cup thyme sprigs, and lemon pieces in cavity of turkey breast.

5. Place turkey, breast side up, on a rack in an aluminum foil-lined roasting pan. Combine oil and melted butter in a small bowl; brush turkey with half of butter mixture. Loosely cover turkey with foil. Bake at 325° for 1 hour.

6. Meanwhile, combine ½ cup maple syrup, apple juice concentrate, and remaining half of butter mixture. Uncover turkey; heavily baste turkey with syrup mixture. Bake 1 hour and 45 more minutes or until a meat thermometer registers 170°, quickly basting with maple syrup mixture every 15 minutes, and shielding with aluminum foil during last 30 minutes of baking. Remove from oven; let stand 10 minutes. Place turkey on a serving platter. Arrange Currant-Stuffed Baked Apples on platter. Garnish, if desired.

Maple-Brined Turkey Breast With Currant-Stuffed Baked Apples

Currant-Stuffed Baked Apples

Makes 12 servings • Hands-On Time: 26 min. • Total Time: 56 min.

- 12 small Braeburn apples (5 lb.)
- ¾ cup firmly packed light brown sugar
- ¾ cup finely chopped walnuts or pecans, toasted
- ½ cup dried currants
- ⅓ cup butter, softened
- 2 tsp. ground cinnamon
- 6 (6-inch) cinnamon sticks, broken in half
- ⅓ cup butter, melted

1. Preheat oven to 375°. Remove apple cores to within ½-inch of bottom of each apple. Using a paring knife or grapefruit knife, increase holes in apples to about 1 inch wide and to within ½ inch from bottom. Arrange apples in a roasting pan.

2. Combine brown sugar and next 4 ingredients, stirring well. Stuff apples with brown sugar mixture, pressing gently to pack; push 1 cinnamon stick into filling of each apple to within ½ inch of bottom. Drizzle melted butter over apples.

3. Add boiling water to pan to depth of ½ inch. Bake, uncovered, at 375° for 30 to 35 minutes or just until apples are tender.

Note: If you're working with one oven, we recommend preparing the stuffed apples first, and then reheating them when the turkey is done.

Sidekicks

Delicious accompaniments that could
steal the spotlight at any meal.

Spiked Apricot-Cranberry Sauce

 make ahead

Spiked Apricot-Cranberry Sauce

Makes 6 cups • Hands-On Time: 22 min. • Total Time: 4 hr., 22 min.

Sweet dessert wine makes a splash in this tart cranberry sauce.
We recommend spooning the sauce over a block of cream cheese
or sliced ham.

- 2 cups sweet white wine
- 1 cup dried apricots, coarsely chopped
- ½ cup sugar
- 2 Tbsp. honey
- 1 tsp. lemon zest
- 1 vanilla bean, split lengthwise
- 2 (12-oz.) packages fresh or frozen cranberries, thawed
- 2 Anjou pears, peeled and coarsely chopped

1. Combine first 5 ingredients in a Dutch oven. Scrape vanilla
bean seeds into mixture; add vanilla bean pod. Bring to a boil
over medium-high heat, stirring occasionally. Reduce heat, and
simmer, uncovered, 5 minutes, stirring often.
2. Increase heat to medium-high; add cranberries and pear.
Bring mixture to a boil. Reduce heat, and simmer, stirring often,
10 minutes or until cranberry skins begin to split and mixture
begins to thicken. Remove from heat, and cool completely.
Remove and discard vanilla bean pod. Cover sauce, and chill
4 hours. Store in refrigerator up to 1 week.

Note: We tested with sweet Riesling White wine.

make ahead

Brussels Sprouts with Spicy Pecans

Makes 8 servings • Hands-On Time: 6 min. • Total Time: 42 min.,
including pecans

Bake the sugared pecans ahead and store them in an airtight
container. Try not to start nibbling until after the Brussels
sprouts are roasted.

- 2 lb. Brussels sprouts
- 2 Tbsp. olive oil
- ½ tsp. salt
- ½ tsp. freshly ground pepper
- Spicy Pecans

1. Preheat oven to 450°. Remove discolored leaves from Brussels
sprouts. Cut off stem ends, and cut in half lengthwise. Toss
Brussels sprouts with oil, salt, and pepper on a large rimmed
baking sheet. Roast at 450° for 22 to 24 minutes, stirring after
20 minutes. Toss with Spicy Pecans; serve immediately.

Brussels Sprouts with Spicy Pecans

Spicy Pecans

Makes 1 cup • Hands-On Time: 1 min. • Total Time: 14 min.

- 1 Tbsp. butter
- 2 Tbsp. sugar
- 1 Tbsp. orange juice
- ¼ tsp. ground cinnamon
- ¼ tsp. ground red pepper
- 1 cup pecan halves

1. Preheat oven to 350°. Melt butter in a large skillet over medium heat; stir in sugar and next 3 ingredients. Cook 1 minute. Stir in pecans; cook 30 seconds, tossing to coat. Remove from heat. Spread pecans on a lightly greased baking sheet. Bake at 350° for 12 minutes, stirring after 10 minutes. Cool completely. Store in an airtight container up to 3 days.

editor's favorite ~ quick & easy

Pan-Sautéed Grape Tomatoes with Mozzarella Cream

Makes 4 servings • Hands-On Time: 17 min. • Total Time: 17 min.

Grape tomatoes maintain their premium quality year-round—that's why we think you'll enjoy this alternative to the more standard of Christmas holiday side dishes. These tomatoes are especially tasty with beef tenderloin.

- 2 Tbsp. olive oil
- 2 pt. grape tomatoes
- 1 large shallot, minced
- 2 Tbsp. dry white wine
- 1 Tbsp. chopped fresh thyme
- 1 tsp. kosher salt
- ½ tsp. freshly ground pepper
- 1 Tbsp. butter
- 1 (8- or 16-oz.) container fresh mozzarella cheese in whey
- 1 Tbsp. olive oil
- ¼ tsp. kosher salt
- ¼ tsp. freshly ground pepper
- 1 garlic clove
- Garnishes: freshly ground pepper, fresh thyme sprigs

Pan-Sautéed Grape Tomatoes with Mozzarella Cream

1. Sauté tomatoes and shallot in 2 Tbsp. hot oil in a large skillet over medium-high heat 4 minutes or until tomatoes begin to burst and skins are blistered. Gently press half of tomatoes with back of a spoon to release juices.

2. Add wine and next 3 ingredients to pan, scraping bottom of pan to loosen any browned bits. Add butter; simmer 5 minutes.

3. Drain mozzarella, reserving ¼ cup liquid. Measure 2 oz. mozzarella; reserve remaining mozzarella for another use. Process 2 oz. mozzarella, reserved liquid, 1 Tbsp. oil, and next 3 ingredients in a food processor 20 seconds or just until smooth.

4. Spoon tomatoes onto individual serving plates; drizzle with mozzarella cream. Garnish, if desired.

Cheese Soufflé-Topped Broccoli

Makes 8 servings • Hands-On Time: 15 min. • Total Time: 54 min.

- 2 (12-oz.) packages fresh broccoli florets
- ½ tsp. salt, divided
- ¼ tsp. freshly ground black pepper
- 3 Tbsp. butter
- 3 Tbsp. all-purpose flour
- 1 cup milk
- ¼ tsp. ground red pepper
- 1½ cups (6 oz.) shredded Gruyère cheese
- 6 large eggs

1. Preheat oven to 375°. Cook broccoli according to package directions in microwave. Combine broccoli, ¼ tsp. salt, and black pepper in a large bowl. Set aside.

2. Meanwhile, melt butter in a heavy saucepan over medium-low heat; whisk in flour until smooth. Cook 1 minute, whisking constantly. Gradually whisk in milk; cook over medium heat, whisking constantly, 2 to 3 minutes or until thickened and bubbly. Add remaining ¼ tsp. salt, red pepper, and cheese, stirring until smooth. Remove from heat.

3. Separate egg yolks and whites into 2 medium bowls. Whisk egg yolks until thick and pale. Slowly whisk one-third of hot cheese sauce into egg yolks, beating until blended. Add yolk mixture to remaining hot cheese sauce, stirring constantly.

4. Beat egg whites at high speed with an electric handheld mixer until stiff peaks form. Gently fold beaten egg whites into egg yolk mixture. Spoon half of broccoli into a lightly greased 2-qt. baking dish. Spoon half of cheese sauce over broccoli. Repeat procedure with remaining broccoli and cheese sauce. Bake at 375° for 15 minutes or until browned and puffed.

Leek and Wild Rice Tart

editor's favorite

Leek and Wild Rice Tart

Makes 8 servings • Hands-On Time: 19 min. • Total Time: 49 min.

½ (14.1-oz.) package refrigerated piecrusts
2 medium leeks
1 (2.75-oz.) package quick-cooking wild rice
¼ cup butter
1 cup heavy cream
1 tsp. Dijon mustard
½ tsp. salt
¼ tsp. freshly ground pepper
⅛ tsp. ground nutmeg
2 large eggs
2 cups (8 oz.) shredded Gruyère cheese

1. Preheat oven to 450°. Roll piecrust into a 13-inch circle on a lightly floured surface. Fit into a 10-inch tart pan with removable bottom; fold edges under, and press into fluted edges. Prick bottom and sides of piecrust with a fork. Bake at 450° for 10 minutes or until lightly browned. Remove to a wire rack, and let cool while preparing filling. Reduce oven temperature to 350°.

2. Remove and discard root ends and dark green tops of leeks. Cut in half lengthwise, and rinse thoroughly under cold running water to remove grit and sand. Thinly slice leeks.

3. Cook rice according to package directions.

4. Meanwhile, melt butter in a large skillet over medium heat; add leeks, and sauté 3 to 5 minutes or until tender.

5. Whisk together whipping cream and next 5 ingredients in a large bowl; stir in cooked rice, leeks, and 1 cup cheese. Sprinkle remaining 1 cup cheese over baked piecrust. Pour leek-and-rice mixture into piecrust. Bake at 350° for 30 minutes or until lightly browned and set.

Roasted Fennel, Sweet Potatoes, and Onion

Makes 4 to 6 servings • Hands-On Time: 10 min. • Total Time: 45 min.

A sprinkling of turbinado sugar adds subtle sweetness to this trio of roasted vegetables. This side makes a nice accompaniment with pork, beef, or poultry.

- 2 fennel bulbs
- 2 medium-size sweet potatoes, peeled and cut into 1-inch cubes (about 12 oz. each)
- 1 large onion, cut into ½-inch-thick wedges
- ¼ cup olive oil
- 2 Tbsp. turbinado sugar
- ½ tsp. kosher salt
- ¼ tsp. freshly ground pepper
- 1 Tbsp. chopped fresh thyme
- 1 tsp. chopped fresh rosemary

1. Preheat oven to 450°. Trim stalks from fennel bulbs. Cut bulbs lengthwise into ½-inch-thick wedges. Combine fennel, sweet potato, onion, and oil on a large rimmed baking sheet; toss well. Sprinkle evenly with sugar, salt, and pepper.
2. Bake at 450° for 25 minutes without stirring. Sprinkle vegetables with chopped herbs; stir gently, turning vegetables. Bake 10 more minutes or until vegetables are browned and tender.

Roasted Lemon, Fig, and Pancetta Dressing

Roasted Lemon, Fig, and Pancetta Dressing

Makes 8 to 10 servings • Hands-On Time: 23 min. • Total Time: 1 hr., 28 min.

There's plenty of bold Italian flavor blended into this tangy rustic dressing. Top it with gravy, if desired.

- 2 lemons, sliced (about ¼ inch thick)
- 1 Tbsp. olive oil
- 8 oz. pancetta, chopped
- 1 large onion, chopped
- 1 (16-oz.) crusty Italian bread loaf, cut into 1-inch cubes
- 1 cup chopped dried figs
- 3 cups chicken broth
- 1 Tbsp. chopped fresh rosemary
- 1 Tbsp. chopped fresh thyme
- 1 tsp. kosher salt
- ½ tsp. freshly ground pepper
- 3 large eggs

1. Preheat oven to 450°. Arrange lemon slices in a single layer on a rimmed baking sheet; drizzle with oil. Bake at 450° for 20 minutes or until edges of lemons are browned. Cool on baking sheet. Reduce oven temperature to 375°.
2. Meanwhile, cook pancetta in a skillet over medium heat 10 minutes or until crisp; remove pancetta, reserving drippings in skillet. Sauté onion in drippings 5 minutes or until tender.
3. Finely chop roasted lemon slices. Combine bread cubes, pancetta, onion, figs, and chopped lemon, stirring well. Whisk together broth and remaining ingredients; pour over bread mixture, tossing well. Spoon mixture into a lightly greased 13- x 9-inch baking dish.
4. Bake, uncovered, at 375° for 45 minutes or until browned and set.

Herbed Pommes Anna

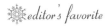
editor's favorite

Herbed Pommes Anna

Makes 8 servings • Hands-On Time: 29 min. • Total Time: 1 hr., 29 min.

Use a well-seasoned cast-iron skillet for this French potato cake.

- 2½ lb. baking potatoes, peeled and very thinly sliced (about ⅛ inch)
- 1 Tbsp. chopped fresh parsley
- 1 tsp. fresh thyme leaves
- 2 Tbsp. olive oil
- ¼ cup butter, melted
- ¾ tsp. salt, divided
- ¾ tsp. freshly ground pepper, divided
- ⅛ tsp. ground nutmeg, divided
- ¼ cup freshly grated Parmigiano-Reggiano cheese
- Garnish: fresh thyme

1. Preheat oven to 425°. Rinse potato slices, and pat dry with paper towels; set aside. Stir together parsley and thyme leaves in a small bowl.

2. Heat oil in a 10-inch cast-iron skillet or ovenproof heavy skillet over medium heat; remove from heat. Carefully arrange a single layer of potato slices (about one-third of potato slices), slightly overlapping, in a circular pattern in skillet. Brush potatoes with 2 Tbsp. melted butter; sprinkle with 2 tsp. herb mixture, ¼ tsp. salt, ¼ tsp. pepper, and a pinch of nutmeg. Repeat layers once. Top with remaining potatoes; sprinkle with remaining ¼ tsp. each salt and pepper, and pinch of nutmeg. Press firmly to pack. Tightly cover potatoes with lightly greased aluminum foil, placing foil directly on surface of potatoes.

3. Bake at 425° for 30 minutes. Uncover and bake 30 more minutes or until top is crisp and browned. Loosen edges of potatoes using a spatula. Invert potatoes onto a serving plate, and sprinkle with cheese. Cut into wedges. Garnish, if desired.

Bite-Size DESSERTS

Good things come in small packages, and it's especially
true with these festive desserts.

Chocolate-Praline
Sundae Shots

Fruitcake-Bourbon Custard Dessert Shots

quick & easy

Chocolate-Praline Sundae Shots

Makes 12 servings • Hands-On Time: 11 min. • Total Time: 23 min.

Use vintage shot glasses for serving these mini indulgences. Bake the candied pecans ahead, and assemble desserts in a snap.

- 1 Tbsp. brown sugar
- 1 tsp. butter, melted
- 12 pecan halves
- 2½ cups butter pecan ice cream
- ½ cup hot fudge sauce

1. Preheat oven to 350°. Combine brown sugar and butter in a small bowl, stirring well. Add pecans; toss to coat. Spread pecans on an ungreased baking sheet. Bake at 350° for 12 minutes. Cool completely.

2. Using a 1 Tbsp. cookie scoop, place 2 ice cream scoops into each of 12 chilled shot glasses or other tiny dessert glasses. Top each dessert with 2 tsp. room-temperature hot fudge sauce and either a praline pecan half or chopped praline pecan. Serve immediately.

make ahead

Fruitcake-Bourbon Custard Dessert Shots

Makes 12 servings • Hands-On Time: 46 min. • Total Time: 3 hr., 26 min., including custard

Christmas means Mimi's bourbon-soaked fruitcake and boiled custard to Test Kitchen Director Elizabeth Austin. This updated twist brings a small bite of fruitcake layered with decadent spiked custard in a delicate cordial glass.

- ½ cup chopped dates
- ½ cup raisins
- ½ cup chopped candied pineapple
- ⅓ cup orange juice
- ¼ cup dried apricots
- ½ cup butter, softened
- ½ cup firmly packed light brown sugar
- 3 large eggs
- 1¼ cups all-purpose flour
- ½ tsp. baking soda
- ¼ tsp. salt
- ½ cup chopped pecans
- 2 tsp. orange zest
- ½ cup bourbon
- Vanilla Bean-Bourbon Custard
- Sweetened whipped cream

1. Combine first 5 ingredients in a medium bowl; cover and let stand 30 minutes.

2. Preheat oven to 325°. Beat butter at medium speed with an electric mixer until creamy; gradually add sugar, beating until blended. Add eggs, 1 at a time, beating until blended after each addition.

3. Combine flour, baking soda, and salt; gradually add flour mixture to butter mixture, beating until blended. Stir in pecans and orange zest.

4. Drain fruit mixture; discard orange juice. Fold fruit mixture into batter. Spoon batter into a lightly greased 8-inch square pan.

5. Bake at 325° for 40 minutes or until a wooden pick inserted in center comes out clean. Poke holes in warm cake with a wooden skewer; pour bourbon over cake, allowing it to seep into holes. Cool completely on a wire rack (about 1 hour).

6. Coarsely crumble half of fruitcake (reserving remaining fruitcake for another use). Layer fruitcake and Vanilla Bean-Bourbon Custard in 4-oz. cordial glasses or shot glasses. Top with whipped cream.

Vanilla Bean-Bourbon Custard

Makes 3 cups • Hands-On Time: 17 min. • Total Time: 2 hr., 17 min.

- ½ cup sugar
- 3 Tbsp. cornstarch
- ¼ tsp. salt
- 2¼ cups milk
- 3 egg yolks
- 3 Tbsp. bourbon
- 1 Tbsp. butter
- 1 tsp. vanilla bean paste or vanilla extract

1. Combine sugar, cornstarch, and salt in a large saucepan; whisk in milk. Cook, whisking constantly, over medium heat 7 minutes or until mixture comes to a boil; boil 1 minute.

2. Whisk egg yolks until thick and pale. Gradually stir about one-fourth of hot milk mixture into yolks; add yolk mixture to remaining hot milk mixture, stirring constantly. Bring mixture to a boil, and cook 3 minutes, whisking constantly. Remove from heat; stir in bourbon, butter, and vanilla. Cover and chill 2 to 24 hours. Whisk custard until smooth before assembling desserts.

make ahead

Baby Bananas Foster Cheesecakes

Makes 3 dozen • Hands-On Time: 24 min. • Total Time: 5 hr., 12 min.

Perfect for a holiday pickup dessert, these one-bite cheesecakes deliver all the goodness of traditional Bananas Foster.

- ¾ cup cinnamon graham cracker crumbs (about 4 sheets)
- ¼ cup finely chopped pecans
- ¼ cup butter, melted
- 1 (8-oz.) package cream cheese, softened
- ⅓ cup firmly packed light brown sugar
- 2 large eggs
- 2 Tbsp. sour cream
- 2 Tbsp. dark rum, divided
- ½ tsp. ground cinnamon
- 3 medium bananas
- ½ cup caramel topping

1. Preheat oven to 325°. Stir together graham cracker crumbs, pecans, and butter in a bowl. Press crumb mixture into bottom of 3 (12-cup) miniature muffin pans. Bake at 325° for 8 minutes; let cool.

2. Beat cream cheese at medium speed with an electric mixer until creamy. Gradually add brown sugar, beating just until blended. Add eggs, 1 at a time, beating just until yellow disappears after each addition. Stir in sour cream, 1 Tbsp. rum, and cinnamon.

3. Mash 1 banana; add mashed banana to cream cheese mixture, beating at low speed just until blended. Spoon cream cheese batter into prepared crust in pans, filling full.

Baby Bananas Foster Cheesecakes

4. Bake at 325° for 18 minutes or until set. Remove cheesecakes from oven; cool completely in pans on a wire rack (about 15 minutes). Cover and chill 4 hours.

5. Heat caramel topping in a saucepan over low heat 2 to 3 minutes. Remove from heat; add remaining 1 Tbsp. rum. Slice remaining 2 bananas into 36 slices (about ¼ inch thick); add to caramel sauce, stirring to coat.

6. Remove cheesecakes from pans. Place 1 caramel-coated banana slice on each cheesecake. Arrange cheesecakes on a serving platter.

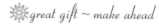

great gift ~ make ahead

German Chocolate Cake Truffles

Makes 8½ dozen • Hands-On Time: 58 min. • Total Time: 2 hr., 58 min.

Whether you call these truffles or cake balls, they're easy to make and fun to dip. Drizzle with white icing (see cover) or sprinkle with sanding sugar for alternate garnishes.

- 1 (18.25-oz.) package German chocolate cake mix
- 1 (16-oz.) container milk chocolate ready-to-spread frosting
- 2 cups toasted coconut, divided
- 1¾ cups toasted finely chopped pecans, divided
  Wax paper
- 4 (7-oz.) containers milk chocolate dipping chocolate
  Candy dipping fork
  Paper or aluminum foil baking cups

1. Prepare and bake cake mix according to package directions in a lightly greased 13- x 9-inch pan. Let cool completely in pan (about 30 minutes).

2. Crumble cake into a large bowl. Scoop frosting by spoonfuls over cake crumbs. Sprinkle with 1 cup each coconut and pecans; stir gently just until thoroughly blended. Using a cookie scoop, scoop cake mixture into 1¼-inch balls; roll in hands, and place balls on wax paper-lined baking sheets. Cover and chill 1 hour.

3. Meanwhile, combine remaining 1 cup coconut and ¾ cup pecans; stir well. Melt dipping chocolate, 1 container at a time, according to package directions; dip chilled balls in melted chocolate, using candy dipping fork and allowing excess chocolate to drip off. Place coated truffles on wax paper-lined baking sheets. Sprinkle tops with coconut-pecan mixture; chill 30 minutes or until set. Place truffles in baking cups.

Note: We tested with Duncan Hines German Chocolate Cake Mix, Betty Crocker Frosting, and Baker's Real Milk Chocolate Dipping Chocolate.

German Chocolate Cake
Truffles

Maple-Walnut Blondie
Stacks

Maple-Walnut Blondie Stacks

Makes 3 dozen • Hands-On Time: 32 min. • Total Time: 2 hr., 44 min., including frosting

A popular national restaurant chain serves a blonde brownie à la mode with a maple-walnut butter sauce. Our recipe has all the same appeal stacked up in one brownie bite.

⅓ cup butter, softened
¾ cup firmly packed light brown sugar
2 large eggs
1 tsp. vanilla extract
¾ cup all-purpose flour
¾ tsp. baking powder
⅛ tsp. salt
⅓ cup finely chopped, toasted walnuts
⅓ cup coarsely crushed hard butter-toffee candies
Maple-Brown Sugar Frosting
Garnishes: additional coarsely crushed hard butter-toffee candies; chopped, toasted walnuts

1. Preheat oven to 350°. Line bottom and sides of an 8-inch square pan with aluminum foil, allowing 2 to 3 inches to extend over sides; lightly grease foil. Set aside.

2. Beat butter and sugar in a large bowl at medium speed with an electric mixer until creamy. Add eggs, 1 at a time, beating after each addition and scraping down sides of bowl. Stir in vanilla.

3. Combine flour, baking powder, and salt in a small bowl, stirring well. Gradually add flour mixture to butter mixture, beating just until blended. Stir in ⅓ cup each walnuts and crushed toffee candies. Spread batter into prepared pan.

4. Bake at 350° for 22 to 25 minutes or until a wooden pick inserted in center comes out with a few moist crumbs. Cool in pan on a wire rack 15 minutes.

5. Lift warm uncut brownies from pan, using foil sides as handles; place on a cutting board. Remove foil; cool uncut brownies completely (about 1 hour). Cut brownies into 4 equal portions. Cut each portion in half horizontally.

6. Spread ¼ cup Maple-Brown Sugar Frosting onto each of 4 brownie portions; top with remaining 4 brownie portions. Cut each stack into 9 pieces. (We recommend using an electric knife.)

7. Spoon remaining frosting into a zip-top plastic freezer bag. Snip 1 corner of bag to make a small hole. Pipe about 1 tsp. frosting onto each brownie stack. Garnish, if desired.

Maple-Brown Sugar Frosting

Makes 2 cups • Hands-On Time: 20 min. • Total Time: 35 min.

- 1 cup firmly packed light brown sugar
- ½ cup evaporated milk
- ⅓ cup butter
- 2 Tbsp. light corn syrup
- 3 cups powdered sugar
- 2 Tbsp. maple syrup
- 1 tsp. vanilla extract

1. Combine first 4 ingredients in a medium saucepan; cook over medium-low heat, stirring constantly, 7 minutes. Bring to a boil over medium-low heat; cook 5 minutes over medium-low heat, stirring constantly. Remove from heat; stir in powdered sugar, syrup, and vanilla. Cool in pan 15 minutes.

2. Transfer warm frosting mixture to a mixing bowl. Beat at medium-high speed with an electric mixer until smooth and spreading consistency (about 8 to 10 minutes).

Creole Calas with Spiced Honey Marmalade

Makes 8 servings • Hands-On Time: 20 min. • Total Time: 20 min., including marmalade

Straight from the French Quarter in New Orleans, calas are a Creole tradition. Served alongside honey marmalade and a dollop of whipped cream, these rice-based fritters make a light dessert that's perfect for sharing.

- Vegetable oil
- 3 cups cooked rice
- ½ cup plus 1 Tbsp. all-purpose flour
- ½ cup sugar
- 1 Tbsp. baking powder
- ¼ tsp. salt
- ¼ tsp. ground nutmeg
- 3 large eggs
- 1 Tbsp. vanilla extract
- ½ cup sugar
- 1 tsp. ground cinnamon
- Spiced Honey Marmalade
- Sweetened whipped cream (optional)

1. Pour oil to a depth of 3 inches into a Dutch oven; heat to 360° over medium-high heat.

2. Meanwhile, combine rice and next 5 ingredients in a large bowl. Whisk together eggs and vanilla; add to rice mixture, and stir just until blended.

3. Drop batter by scant Tbsp. into hot oil, and fry, in batches, 2 minutes on each side or until golden brown. Drain on paper towels.

4. Meanwhile, combine ½ cup sugar and cinnamon in a small bowl. Roll hot calas in cinnamon sugar, coating well. Serve hot with Spiced Honey Marmalade and, if desired, whipped cream.

Note: We tested with Success Rice, cooked according to package directions.

Spiced Honey Marmalade

Makes ¾ cup • Hands-On Time: 2 min. • Total Time: 2 min.

- ½ cup orange marmalade
- ¼ cup honey
- ⅛ tsp. ground cloves

1. Combine all ingredients in a small saucepan. Cook over medium heat 1 minute or until melted. Remove from heat; serve hot.

Creole Calas with Spiced Honey Marmalade

great gift

Little Gingerbread Scones

Makes 14 servings • Hands-On Time: 10 min. • Total Time: 38 min.

Gingerbread flavor is a big hit in these warm, sugar-crusted scones. Scones can be reheated, 1 at a time, for 20 seconds in the microwave.

2½ cups all-purpose flour
⅔ cup firmly packed dark brown sugar
1 Tbsp. baking powder
2½ tsp. ground ginger
1 tsp. ground cinnamon
½ tsp. salt
3 Tbsp. crystallized ginger, finely chopped and divided
½ cup cold butter, cut into pieces
¾ cup plus 2 Tbsp. whipping cream, divided
3 Tbsp. molasses
1 Tbsp. vanilla extract
2 Tbsp. turbinado sugar
Parchment paper

1. Preheat oven to 425°. Combine first 6 ingredients in a large bowl; stir in 2 Tbsp. crystallized ginger. Cut butter into flour mixture with a pastry blender until crumbly and mixture resembles small peas. Combine ¾ cup plus 1 Tbsp. whipping cream, molasses, and vanilla; add to dry ingredients, stirring with a fork just until dry ingredients are moistened.
2. Knead dough in bowl 4 or 5 times until dough holds together. Combine turbinado sugar and remaining 1 Tbsp. crystallized ginger; stir well.
3. Drop dough by ¼ cupfuls onto parchment paper-lined baking sheets. Brush tops with remaining 1 Tbsp. cream; sprinkle with turbinado-ginger mixture.
4. Bake at 425° for 16 minutes or until a wooden pick inserted in center comes out clean.

Note: For more shapely scone wedges, we recommend using a nonstick aluminum mini scone pan. Find pan online through The Baker's Catalogue. Proceed with recipe as directed. Divide dough evenly into scone pan greased with shortening, filling triangles full. Bake at 425° for 18 minutes. Makes 16 triangular scones.

Meyer Lemon-Glazed Doughnut Holes

Makes 3 dozen • Hands-On Time: 22 min. • Total Time: 1 hr., 58 min., including glaze

Let guests dip these in the tangy glaze.

1 (¼-oz.) envelope active dry yeast
¼ cup sugar, divided
¼ cup milk
½ tsp. salt
1 large egg, lightly beaten
1½ cups all-purpose flour
Vegetable oil
Meyer Lemon Glaze

1. Combine yeast, ¼ cup warm water (100° to 110°), and 1 tsp. sugar in a 1-cup glass measuring cup; let stand 5 minutes.
2. Cook milk in a heavy nonaluminum saucepan over medium heat, stirring constantly 30 seconds or until bubbles appear (do not boil); remove from heat. Combine milk, remaining sugar, and salt in a large bowl, stirring until sugar dissolves. Let stand until temperature reaches 105° to 115°. Add egg and yeast mixture to milk mixture; stir well. Gradually stir in enough flour to make a sticky dough.
3. Turn dough out onto a lightly floured surface, and knead until smooth and elastic (about 5 minutes). Place in a well-greased bowl, turning to grease top.
4. Cover loosely with plastic wrap, and let rise in a warm place (85°), free from drafts, 1 hour or until almost doubled in bulk.
5. Punch down dough; let stand 5 minutes. Shape into 36 (¾-inch-thick) balls; place on a parchment paper-lined baking sheet. Cover loosely with plastic wrap, and let rise in a warm place (85°),15 to 20 minutes or until almost doubled in bulk.
6. Preheat oven to 225°. Pour oil to depth of 2 inches into a large heavy skillet; heat to 350°. Fry doughnuts, in batches, 45 seconds on each side or until golden brown. Remove with a slotted spoon; drain on paper towels. Keep doughnuts warm on a wire rack in a pan in a 225° oven up to 30 minutes.
7. Dip warm doughnuts in Meyer Lemon Glaze. Drain on a wire rack over a baking sheet. Serve warm.

Note: We tested with White Lily All-Purpose Flour.

Meyer Lemon Glaze

Makes ¾ cup • Hands-On Time: 2 min. • Total Time: 2 min.

4 cups powdered sugar
2 tsp. Meyer lemon zest
6 Tbsp. fresh Meyer lemon juice

1. Combine all ingredients in a bowl, whisking until smooth.

Mini Macadamia-Coconut
Cream Pies

☃ editor's favorite

Mini Macadamia-Coconut Cream Pies

Makes 32 servings • Hands-On Time: 39 min. • Total Time: 2 hr., 49 min.

This clever take on coconut cream pie has a coconut cookie crust and a silky filling made with coconut milk.

2 (10-oz.) packages soft coconut macaroon cookies
1 egg white, beaten
⅓ cup very finely chopped macadamia nuts
⅓ cup sugar
2½ Tbsp. cornstarch
1 (13.5-oz.) can coconut milk
2 egg yolks
½ tsp. vanilla extract
⅛ tsp. salt
½ cup sweetened flaked coconut, toasted

1. Preheat oven to 350°. Carefully press cookies into bottom of 3 (12-cup) lightly greased miniature muffin pans. Brush with beaten egg white; sprinkle evenly with nuts, gently pressing nuts into cookies.

2. Bake at 350° for 12 minutes or until lightly browned. Cool in pans on wire racks 10 minutes; remove from pans to wire racks, and cool completely (about 20 minutes).

3. Combine sugar and cornstarch in a heavy saucepan. Whisk together coconut milk and egg yolks. Gradually whisk egg mixture into sugar mixture; bring to a simmer over medium heat, whisking constantly. Cook, whisking constantly, 3 minutes. Remove from heat; stir in vanilla and salt.

4. Place pan in ice water for 10 minutes; whisk custard occasionally until cool. Spoon custard filling into prepared crusts. Place heavy-duty plastic wrap directly on surface of custard (to prevent a film from forming); chill at least 2 hours. Sprinkle with toasted coconut before serving.

Note: We tested with Archway Coconut Macaroon Cookies.

Pancake PERFECTION

This morning fill-me-up isn't just for breakfast anymore. From savory to sweet, pancakes are a crowd-pleaser any way you stack 'em.

editor's favorite ~ quick & easy

Sweet Potato Pancakes with Toasted Hazelnut Syrup

Makes 11 (5-inch) pancakes • Hands-On Time: 16 min. • Total Time: 16 min.

1½ cups whole wheat buttermilk pancake mix
½ tsp. ground cinnamon
1½ cups milk
1 large egg
¼ cup butter, melted
1 cup mashed sweet potato
1½ cups maple syrup
½ cup chopped toasted hazelnuts
2 Tbsp. butter
1 vanilla bean, split lengthwise
Garnish: toasted hazelnuts

1. Combine pancake mix and cinnamon in a large bowl. Stir together milk and egg; add to pancake mix, stirring until blended. Stir in melted butter. Add sweet potato, stirring just until blended. (Batter will be thick.)
2. Pour about ⅓ cup batter for each pancake onto a hot, lightly greased griddle or large nonstick skillet; spread each into a 5-inch circle. Cook pancakes 3 to 4 minutes or until tops are covered with bubbles and edges look dry and cooked; turn and cook other side 2 to 3 minutes more.
3. Meanwhile, combine syrup, ½ cup chopped hazelnuts, 2 Tbsp. butter, and vanilla bean in a saucepan. Bring to a simmer over medium heat; reduce heat, and keep warm over low heat. Remove and discard vanilla bean before serving.
4. If desired, stack multiple pancakes on a plate with 2 Tbsp. hazelnut syrup mixture between each layer. Spoon more hazelnut syrup over top of stack. Using a sharp knife, cut stack into 4 big wedges; transfer to individual plates. Repeat procedure with remaining pancakes and additional syrup mixture. Garnish wedges, if desired. Serve with remaining syrup mixture.

Note: We tested with Hodgson Mill Whole Wheat Buttermilk Pancake Mix. Cornmeal in the mix contributes a certain rustic appeal.

Bacon Pancakes

Makes about 18 (4-inch) pancakes • Hands-On Time: 29 min. • Total Time: 32 min. (including sauce)

Cornmeal and bacon add distinct texture and savory goodness to these unique cakes. Use fully-cooked bacon for convenience.

2 cups all-purpose flour
⅓ cup plain yellow cornmeal
1 Tbsp. sugar
2 tsp. baking powder
1 tsp. baking soda
¾ tsp. salt
8 cooked bacon slices, crumbled
2 cups milk
2 Tbsp. white vinegar
¼ cup unsalted butter, melted
1 large egg, lightly beaten
Orange-Honey Sauce

1. Combine first 6 ingredients in a large bowl. Stir in bacon. Whisk together milk and vinegar; let stand 3 minutes. Add milk mixture, melted butter, and egg to dry ingredients. Stir with a fork just until blended (batter will be slightly lumpy).
2. Preheat oven to 200°. Pour about ¼ cup batter for each pancake onto a hot, lightly greased griddle or large non-stick skillet over medium heat. Cook pancakes 3 minutes or until tops are covered with bubbles and edges look dry and cooked; turn and cook other side 2 to 3 minutes or until done. Place pancakes in a single layer on a baking sheet, and keep warm in a 200° oven up to 30 minutes. Serve with warm Orange-Honey Sauce.

Orange-Honey Sauce

Makes 1⅓ cups • Hands-On Time: 3 min. • Total Time: 3 min.

1 cup orange marmalade
3 Tbsp. honey
3 Tbsp. butter

1. Combine all ingredients in a saucepan. Cook over medium heat until butter melts, stirring until smooth.

Bacon Pancakes with
Orange-Honey Sauce

Cheesecake Pancake Stacks with Spiced Cranberry Sauce

Kids' Pancakes

Black Forest Pancakes,
page 126

Poppy Seed-Lemon Pancakes,
page 126

Cheesecake Pancake Stacks with Spiced Cranberry Sauce

Makes 14 (4-inch) pancakes • Hands-On Time: 30 min. • Total Time: 40 min.

Find the rich flavors of a classic cheesecake stacked on this breakfast plate.

CHEESECAKE FILLING

- 1 (8-oz.) package cream cheese, softened
- ¼ cup butter, softened
- 3 cups powdered sugar
- 1 tsp. vanilla extract

SPICED CRANBERRY SAUCE

- 2½ cups sugar
- 2 Tbsp. cornstarch
- 1 tsp. pumpkin pie spice
- 1 (12-oz.) package fresh or frozen cranberries, thawed
- 2 Tbsp. butter
- 1 tsp. vanilla extract

PANCAKES

- 2 cups all-purpose flour
- 3 Tbsp. sugar
- 2½ tsp. baking powder
- ¼ tsp. salt
- 1 (3-oz.) package cream cheese, softened
- 1½ cups milk, divided
- 1 large egg
- 2 Tbsp. butter, melted
- 1 tsp. vanilla extract

1. Prepare Cheesecake Filling: Beat cream cheese and butter at medium speed with an electric mixer until smooth; gradually add powdered sugar, beating until blended. Stir in vanilla. Cover and chill.

2. Prepare Spiced Cranberry Sauce: Combine first 3 ingredients in a 3 qt. saucepan; stir well. Stir in cranberries and 2¼ cups water. Bring to a boil over medium heat, stirring constantly; reduce heat, and simmer 8 minutes or until cranberries pop and mixture thickens slightly, mashing berries against sides of pan. Remove from heat; add butter and vanilla, stirring until butter melts.

3. Prepare Pancakes: Stir together flour, sugar, baking powder, and salt in a large bowl; make a well in center of mixture. Beat cream cheese and ¼ cup milk in a small bowl at low speed with an electric mixer until smooth. Gradually add remaining milk, beating at medium speed until smooth. Add egg, melted butter, and vanilla; beat until blended. Add cream cheese mixture to dry ingredients, stirring just until blended. Let batter stand 3 minutes.

4. Pour about ¼ cup batter for each pancake onto a hot, buttered griddle or large nonstick skillet; spread each into a 4-inch circle. Cook pancakes 3 to 4 minutes or until tops are covered with bubbles and edges look dry and cooked; turn and cook 1 to 2 more minutes.

5. For each serving, stack 2 pancakes on individual plates, spreading or piping ¼ cup Cheesecake Filling between pancakes. Top with Spiced Cranberry Sauce. Serve immediately.

Kids' Pancakes

Makes 10 (4-inch) pancakes • Hands-On Time: 16 min. • Total Time: 16 min.

The whole family will enjoy the options that await with this simple pancake recipe. Find a pancake pen online or at a local kitchen shop.

- 1½ cups all-purpose flour
- 1½ Tbsp. sugar
- 1 Tbsp. baking powder
- ¾ tsp. salt
- 1¼ cups milk
- 1½ tsp. vanilla extract
- 1 large egg, lightly beaten
- 3 Tbsp. butter, melted
- Powdered sugar

1. Combine first 4 ingredients in a medium bowl. Stir together milk, vanilla, and egg; add to dry ingredients, stirring just until smooth. Stir in butter.

2. If desired, pour batter into a pancake pen and secure top. Squirt desired shapes onto a hot, lightly greased griddle or large nonstick skillet over medium heat. (Otherwise, pour about ¼ cup batter for each pancake onto griddle or skillet.) Cook pancakes 3 minutes or until tops are covered with bubbles and edges look dry and cooked. Turn and cook other side 3 minutes or until golden. Sprinkle with powdered sugar before serving.

Sprinkle Pancakes: Stir 2½ Tbsp. rainbow candy sprinkles into pancake batter. Prepare recipe as directed. Squirt each pancake with refrigerated instant whipped cream and, if desired, garnish with more sprinkles. Makes 10 (4-inch) pancakes.

 *editor's favorite ~ quick & easy*

Poppy Seed-Lemon Pancakes

(pictured on page 124)

Makes about 13 (4-inch) pancakes • Hands-On Time: 25 min. • Total Time: 30 min.

The delicate flavor pairing of lemon and poppy seeds shines in these buttery, light pancakes. No syrup's necessary, but warmed lemon curd sure makes a delicious finish.

2   cups all-purpose flour
¼   cup sugar
2   Tbsp. poppy seeds
1   Tbsp. baking powder
¼   tsp. baking soda
½   tsp. salt
1   cup milk
¼   cup sour cream
¼   cup butter, melted
1   Tbsp. lemon zest
1   Tbsp. fresh lemon juice
½   tsp. vanilla extract
1   large egg, separated
1   egg white
   Powdered sugar
1   (10-oz.) jar lemon curd (optional)

1. Combine first 6 ingredients in a large bowl. Add milk, next 5 ingredients, and egg yolk, whisking just until blended.
2. Beat 2 egg whites at high speed with an electric mixer until stiff peaks form. Gently fold beaten egg white into batter.
3. Pour about ¼ cup batter for each pancake onto a hot, lightly greased griddle or large nonstick skillet over medium heat. Cook pancakes 3 minutes or until tops are covered with bubbles and edges look dry and cooked; turn and cook other side 2 to 3 minutes more. Sprinkle with powdered sugar. Serve with lemon curd, if desired.

Note: If desired, spoon lemon curd into a large glass measuring cup; cover loosely, and microwave at HIGH 45 seconds to 1 minute, stirring at 15-second intervals. Spoon lemon curd "syrup" over pancakes.

 *quick & easy*

Black Forest Pancakes

(pictured on page 124)

Makes 10 (4-inch) pancakes • Hands-On Time: 5 min. • Total Time: 29 min. (including sauce)

1   cup self-rising flour
¼   cup unsweetened cocoa
¼   cup sugar
1   cup half-and-half
1   large egg, lightly beaten
   Dark Cherry Sauce
   Chocolate syrup
   Sweetened whipped cream

1. Combine first 3 ingredients in a medium bowl, stirring well. Add half-and-half and egg, stirring just until blended.
2. Pour about ¼ cup batter for each pancake onto a hot, buttered griddle or large nonstick skillet. Cook pancakes 2 to 3 minutes on medium-low heat or just until tops are almost covered with bubbles and begin to look dry; turn and cook other side 1 to 2 minutes. (Batter will thicken as it stands, so spread as needed on griddle.)
3. Stack 2 or 3 pancakes on individual plates; spoon Dark Cherry Sauce over each stack. Drizzle with chocolate syrup, and dollop with whipped cream. Serve immediately.

Dark Cherry Sauce

Makes 2½ cups • Hands-On Time: 4 min. • Total Time: 16 min.

¾   cup sugar
2   Tbsp. cornstarch
¼   tsp. ground cinnamon
1   (16-oz.) package dark, sweet frozen cherries, thawed and undrained
1   Tbsp. butter
2   tsp. vanilla extract
1   Tbsp. amaretto liqueur or ⅛ tsp. almond extract

1. Whisk together first 3 ingredients in a large saucepan. Stir in 1 cup water. Bring to a boil over medium heat, stirring constantly, until thickened and bubbly. Stir in cherries, butter, and vanilla; cook over medium heat until butter is melted. Remove from heat; stir in amaretto.

Southwest Cheddar
Pancakes

Southwest Cheddar Pancakes

Makes 12 (4-inch) pancakes • Hands-On Time: 50 min. • Total Time: 50 min.

Who says pancakes have to be sweet? Here's a savory pancake entrée (think chicken and waffles); team this with grilled pork tenderloin, if desired.

1¾ cups self-rising flour
¾ cup buttermilk
⅓ cup vegetable oil
3 large eggs, separated
1 cup (4 oz.) shredded sharp Cheddar cheese
2 green onions, chopped
1 (11-oz.) can yellow corn with red and green bell peppers, drained

Garnishes: salsa and chopped green onions

1. Place flour in a large bowl; make a well in center. Stir together buttermilk, oil, and egg yolks; add to flour, stirring just until moistened.

2. Beat egg whites at high speed with an electric mixer until stiff peaks form; fold into batter. Add cheese, 2 chopped green onions, and corn to batter, stirring just until blended. (Batter will be thick.)

3. Pour about ⅓ cup batter for each pancake onto a hot, lightly greased griddle or large nonstick skillet; spread each into a 4-inch circle. Cook pancakes 3 to 4 minutes or until tops are covered with bubbles and edges look dry and cooked; turn and cook other side 2 minutes or until done. Garnish, if desired.

Extreme Hot Chocolate

Slow Cooker SURPRISES

Less hands-on time for the cook means more time with your guests. These inspired starters, sides and sweets only taste like you spent hours in the kitchen.

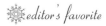
editor's favorite

Extreme Hot Chocolate

Makes 12 cups • Hands-On Time: 6 min. • Total Time: 4 hr., 6 min.

Serve this luxuriously thick treat in small mugs. Big, pillowy toasted marshmallows send it over the top. If desired, keep at WARM setting for up to 2 hours.

- 1 (12-oz.) can evaporated milk
- 1 cup instant nonfat dry milk
- 4½ cups milk
- 3 cups whipping cream
- ⅛ tsp. salt
- 1 (11.5-oz.) package bittersweet chocolate morsels
- 1 (12-oz.) package semisweet chocolate morsels
- 1 (10-oz.) package large marshmallows
- Parchment paper
- 1 Tbsp. vanilla extract
- Coffee liqueur* (optional)

1. Whisk together evaporated milk and dry milk in a 4-qt. slow cooker until smooth. Whisk in milk and next 2 ingredients. Add chocolate morsels. Cover and cook on LOW 4 hours, whisking until smooth after 2 hours.
2. Preheat broiler with oven rack 3 inches from heat. Place 12 marshmallows on a parchment paper-lined baking sheet. Broil 2 minutes or just until toasted. Repeat procedure with desired amount of marshmallows. Stir vanilla into hot chocolate, and ladle into mugs. Stir 1 tablespoon liqueur into each serving, if desired, and top each serving with 1 to 2 toasted marshmallows.

Ultimate Fondue

quick & easy

Ultimate Fondue

Makes 12 to 14 appetizer servings
Hands-On Time: 10 min. • Total Time: 1 hr., 40 min.

Serve this popular dip with chunks of ciabatta bread, large corn chips, or multigrain tortilla chips.

- 1 (8-oz.) package shredded Swiss cheese
- 1 (8-oz.) package shredded mozzarella cheese
- 2 (4-oz.) containers garlic-and-herb spreadable cheese
- ½ cup (2 oz.) shredded Parmesan cheese
- ½ cup heavy cream
- ½ cup mayonnaise
- 1 (10-oz.) package frozen chopped spinach, thawed
- 1 (12-oz.) jar quartered marinated artichoke hearts, drained
- 1 (8-oz.) can sliced water chestnuts, drained
- 1 (7-oz.) jar sliced pimiento, drained

1. Combine first 6 ingredients in a lightly greased 3- or 4-qt. slow cooker.
2. Drain spinach well, pressing between paper towels.
3. Stir spinach, artichokes, and remaining 2 ingredients into cheese mixture. Cover and cook on LOW 1 hour and 30 minutes or until cheese melts, stirring after 45 minutes.

Corn Pudding Soufflé

Makes 8 servings • Hands-On Time: 12 min. • Total Time: 3 hr., 12 min.

- 4   cups frozen baby gold and white whole kernel corn, thawed
- 4   oz. cream cheese, softened
- 1   cup milk
- ½   cup sour cream
- 3   Tbsp. butter, melted
- 2   Tbsp. sugar
- 2   Tbsp. all-purpose flour
- 1½   tsp. baking powder
- 1   tsp. salt
- 4   large eggs
- 1   cup (4 oz.) shredded Monterey Jack cheese

1. Pulse corn 3 times in a food processor until finely chopped. Scrape down sides; add cream cheese and remaining ingredients. Process 30 seconds or just until combined. (Do not puree corn.)

2. Pour corn mixture into a lightly greased 5-qt. oval slow cooker. Cover and cook on LOW 3 hours or until pudding is puffed and browned around edges.

3. Remove insert from slow cooker. Let pudding stand, covered, 10 minutes before serving.

New Year's Day Peppery Peas

Makes 11 servings • Hands-On Time: 7 min. • Total Time: 8 hr., 13 min.

Pull out your frozen pea supply for this well-seasoned good luck dish.

- 4   bacon slices
- 1   large onion, chopped
- 2   cups frozen black-eyed peas
- 2   cups frozen purple hull peas
- 2   cups frozen crowder peas
- 2   cups frozen butter peas
- 2   cups frozen field peas with snaps (do not thaw)
- 2   Tbsp. Asian chili-garlic sauce
- 1½   tsp. freshly ground pepper
- 1   tsp. salt
- 1   (32-oz.) container chicken broth

1. Cook bacon in a large skillet over medium-high heat 6 minutes or until crisp; remove bacon, and drain on paper towels, reserving drippings in skillet. Crumble bacon, and set aside. Sauté onion in drippings 2 minutes.

2. Place sautéed onion, black-eyed peas, and remaining ingredients in a 5-qt. slow cooker; stir. Cover and cook on LOW 8 hours or until peas are tender. Sprinkle with bacon before serving.

Rich Sweet Potatoes with Bourbon

Rich Sweet Potatoes with Bourbon

Makes 10 servings • Hands-On Time: 7 min. • Total Time: 3 hr., 7 min.

These slow cooker spiked sweet potatoes allow your oven to be freed up for other foods during the holiday hustle and bustle.

- ⅔   cup firmly packed dark brown sugar
- ⅓   cup butter, melted
- 1   Tbsp. vanilla bean paste or vanilla extract
- 2   (24-oz.) packages refrigerated mashed sweet potatoes
- 2   large eggs, lightly beaten
- ¼   cup whipping cream
- ¼   cup bourbon
- 2   cups praline pecans

1. Combine first 5 ingredients in a large bowl, stirring until smooth. Stir in cream and bourbon. Spoon sweet potato mixture into a lightly greased 3-qt. slow cooker. Cover and cook on HIGH 3 hours.

2. Stir in ½ cup pecans. Sprinkle remaining 1½ cups pecans over top of sweet potatoes just before serving.

Note: Check a local upscale market during the holiday season for bourbon-praline pecans. Some stores sell these nuts along with bulk items such as specialty candies and dried fruits.

Cranberry Upside-Down Cake

Makes 8 to 10 servings • Hands-On Time: 10 min. • Total Time: 2 hr., 30 min.

Here's a festive twist on traditional pineapple upside-down cake. Serve with sweetened whipped cream to complement the tartness of the cranberries.

1   cup firmly packed light brown sugar
½   cup butter, melted
1   (14-oz.) can whole-berry cranberry sauce
1   (12-oz.) package fresh cranberries
1   (16-oz.) package pound cake mix
¾   cup milk
2   large eggs
½   tsp. almond extract
Vanilla ice cream (optional)

1. Lightly grease a 5-qt. slow cooker. Stir together first 3 ingredients in a small bowl until blended. Pour mixture into prepared slow cooker. Top with cranberries.
2. Beat pound cake mix, milk, and next 2 ingredients at low speed with an electric mixer 30 seconds, scraping bowl constantly. Beat on low speed 2 minutes. Pour batter over

cranberries. Cover and cook on HIGH 2 hours and 10 minutes or until a wooden pick inserted in center comes out clean. Turn off slow cooker; let cake stand, covered, 20 minutes. Invert cake onto a serving platter. Cut into wedges, and serve with ice cream, if desired.

Note: Rotate the insert in your slow cooker during cook time if it's prone to hot spots.

 *editor's favorite*

Bittersweet Fudge Brownie Bread Pudding

Makes 8 to 10 servings • Hands-On Time: 15 min. • Total Time: 3 hr., 25 min.

Two make-ahead steps make this dessert a cinch to put together—bake brownies and tear the bread a day ahead. Serve this luscious pudding warm from the crock with dollops of whipped cream or vanilla ice cream.

1   (20-oz.) package double chocolate brownie mix
8   large eggs
¾   cup sugar
1   Tbsp. vanilla extract or vanilla bean paste
Pinch of salt
3   cups heavy cream
1   (1-lb.) loaf ciabatta bread, cut into 1-inch cubes (about 8 cups)
1   (11.5-oz.) package bittersweet chocolate morsels
1   cup pecan halves, toasted (optional)
1   slow-cooker liner

1. Prepare and bake brownies according to package directions. Cool completely, and cut into 1½-inch chunks to measure 4 cups packed, reserving remaining brownies for another use. Cover and set aside up to 1 day ahead.
2. Whisk together eggs and next 3 ingredients in a large bowl; whisk in cream until blended. Stir in bread and 4 cups brownie chunks. Stir in chocolate morsels and, if desired, nuts.
3. Place liner in a 5-qt. round slow cooker according to manufacturer's instructions. Heavily coat liner with cooking spray. Spoon bread mixture into liner. Cover and cook on HIGH 3 hours or until pudding is set in center, rotating slow cooker insert twice to prevent overbrowning of bottom edge. Turn off slow cooker; let stand, uncovered, 10 minutes. Serve warm.

Note: Your favorite fudgy brownies will also work fine in this recipe. You need just 4 cups of brownie chunks. If in a hurry, pick up brownies at the bakery.

Cranberry Upside-Down Cake

Share

GIVE SOME LOVE AND LAUGHTER
THIS HOLIDAY WITH FROM-SCRATCH
SWEETS AND HOMESPUN GIFTS.

10 Favorite
HOMESPUN CRAFTS FOR GIVING

Rethink holiday giving. The greatest gifts are often the ones you make yourself. From decor to jewelry to whimsical toys, here are some inspired ideas sure to please everyone on your list. See Resources (page 170) to find the materials you'll need.

1. *For the Entertainer*
HOLLY NAPKIN RINGS

Turn inexpensive felt into holiday decor for the table using the simple technique of needle felting.

MATERIALS
felt in assorted colors
rotary cutter and self-healing mat
scissors
ruler
leaf template
small foam balls
felting needle
needle and thread

HOW TO
1. Lay piece of felt flat on mat.

2. Using rotary cutter, cut felt into strips that are 2½" x 6½".

3. Using leaf template, trace leaves onto more felt; cut out with scissors.

4. Pinch leaf and stitch to form "stem."

5. Stitch 2 leaves together at the stem.

6. Cover foam balls with a circular piece of felt large enough to cover it entirely.

7. Use felting needle to push felt into the foam ball until completely smooth.

8. Sew felted ball between leaves.

9. Sew the strip of felt together in back to make a ring.

10. Sew holly to the middle of strips of felt.

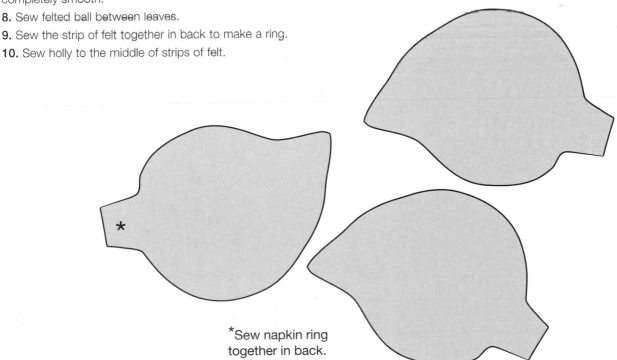

*
*Sew napkin ring together in back.

2. *For the Eco-minded*
MAGAZINE TREES AND PINWHEEL ORNAMENTS

Like vintage accordion-style paper ornaments, these decorations are a whimsical way to recycle catalogs and old magazines.

Magazine Trees

MATERIALS
magazines or catalogs in different dimensions
bone folder
stapler
small hole punch

OPTIONAL
spray paint
spray adhesive
fine glitter

HOW TO
1. Break spine of magazine, making sure pages remain attached.
2. Bring the bottom corner of the first page up and over to the spine so that bottom edge of the page is in line with spine creating a triangular flap.
3. Make the fold crisp and clean with the bone folder.
4. Continue folding each page in an identical manner until all are folded.
5. When complete, begin the second fold by folding the crisp folded edge over and in line with the spine.
6. Continue until all the pages have been folded this second time.

7. When complete, fold the bottom edge of each page under to complete the folding and create a flat-based tree.
8. Staple first and last page together to hold the form of the tree, if needed.

OPTIONAL
1. Spray-paint and let dry completely.
2. Coat lightly with spray adhesive.
3. Sprinkle glitter, shaking off excess; let dry.

Pinwheel Ornaments

HOW TO
1. Tear out several pages from a magazine or catalog.
2. Fold over and under until page is completely folded accordion style.
3. Collapse folds into a flat strip, then fold in half at middle.
4. Staple at middle fold.
5. Cut at open end to desired size.
6. Open the pinwheel, bringing together, and staple to secure.
7. Punch a hole for a ribbon.

OPTIONAL (In a ventilated space)
1. Spray-paint desired color.
2. When dry, coat lightly with spray adhesive.
3. Sprinkle with glitter, shaking off excess; let dry.

1. Bring the corner of a page up and over to meet the spine and make a crisp fold with the bone folder.

2. After all the pages have been folded the first time, make the second fold by folding the crisp folded edge over to the spine and crease.

3. When all pages have been folded a second time, fold the bottom edge under to create a flat-based tree.

3. *For the Host and Hostess*
GLITTERED DEER PLACE CARD HOLDERS

Sparkling diminutive reindeer are sure to become heirlooms of the Christmas table. Box them with a stack of blank cards for the host to fill out for years to come.

MATERIALS
plastic toy deer
paintbrush
craft glue
fine glitter
tray to catch glitter
paper for name card

HOW TO
1. Paint entire deer with craft glue, avoiding eyes, nose, and hooves.
2. Set on tray and sprinkle completely with glitter.
3. When dry, shake off excess glitter.
4. Cut blank name cards to fit between antlers.

4. *For the Beachcomber*
SEASHELL GLITTERED ORNAMENTS

Bedazzle assorted shells in an array of glittery hues. In bowls, on the tree, or as sparkling accents on the table, these shimmering gems of the sea add a bit of glamour to the holidays.

MATERIALS
seashells
small paintbrush
craft glue
fine glitter
tray to catch glitter
ribbon

HOW TO
1. Paint shells completely on front and back with craft glue.
2. Set on tray and sprinkle with glitter until completely covered, shaking off excess.
3. Let dry completely.
4. Add ribbon, if desired.

5. For the Nature Lover
BIRD ORNAMENTS

Perfectly fitting for the holidays, doves are a symbol of peace. Hung from the tree or rafters, these ivory birds-in-flight add meaningful elegance to a room.

MATERIALS
bird templates
felt sheets with coated back
scissors
craft knife
hole punch
ribbon

HOW TO
1. Using the template, trace body and wing shapes onto felt.
2. Cut out shapes with scissors.
3. Make a slit with a craft knife for inserting wing through body.
4. Insert wing into slot in body.
5. Punch hole in top middle of the back above the wing.
6. Thread ribbon through hole and knot for hanging.

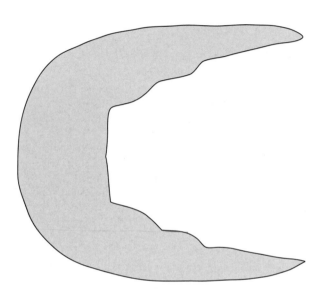

Use a copier to enlarge patterns to desired size

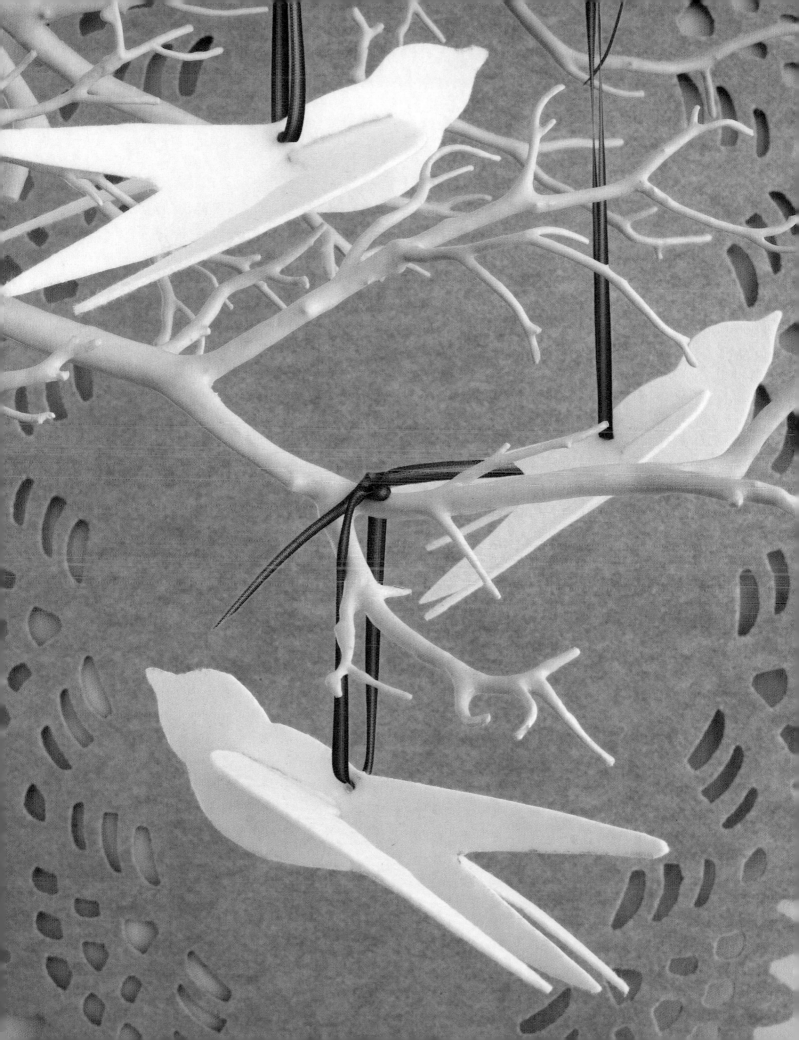

6. *For Students or Office Mates*
CORKBOARD PENCIL CUPS WITH FABRIC-COVERED TACKS

Perfect for office supplies, potted plants, even kitchen utensils and workshop tools, these handy holders are a functional way to keep up with to-dos or display photos.

Corkboard Pencil Cups

MATERIALS
empty cans in different sizes
white spray paint
natural cork liner

HOW TO
1. Clean cans and remove labels.
2. Paint inside and outside of can with spray paint; let dry.
3. Wrap cork around can 3 times for ample thickness.
4. Measure and cut cork to width and height of can with rotary cutter on self-healing mat.
5. Peel paper backing from cork and press onto can to secure as it is rolled onto can.

Fabric-Covered Tacks

MATERIALS
covered button kit
fabric of choice
flat-topped thumbtacks
hot glue gun

HOW TO
1. Follow instructions on back of covered button kit to cover with fabric (if button backs have raised hooks, clip them off using wire cutters).
2. Hot-glue thumbtacks to button backs.
3. Let glue dry completely.

7. For the Seamstress or Crafter
EMBROIDERY RING ORNAMENTS

Following the designs of holiday tea towels or napkins makes these embroidered ornaments a cinch to make and a pleasure to receive.

MATERIALS
holiday towels, napkins, or fabric of choice
embroidery rings
scissors
embroidery needle
embroidery floss

HOW TO
1. Cut fabric into squares 1" larger than the inside ring.
2. Stretch fabric over embroidery ring with design centered as desired.
3. Screw tight to hold fabric in place.
4. Cut off excess fabric.
5. Hot-glue back with both rings and fabric in place.
6. Sew over pattern on top of fabric.

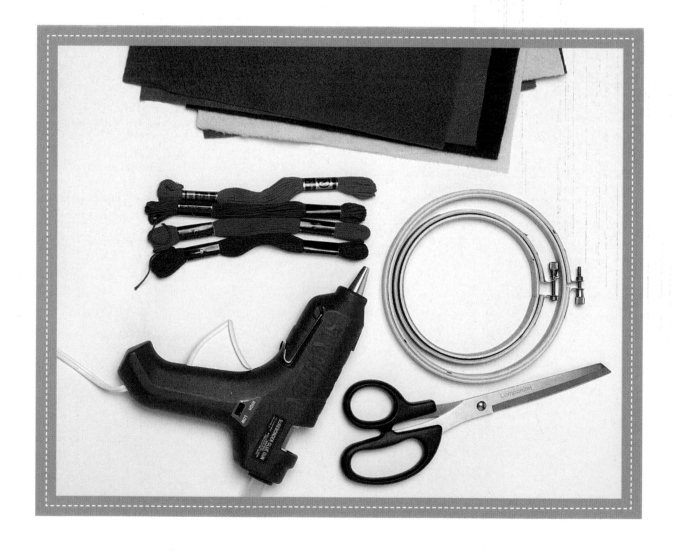

8. *For the Fashionista*
SHRINK PLASTIC "JEWELS"

Shrink plastic is an inexpensive and fun-to-use craft medium that can be made into one-of-a-kind necklaces, earrings, or ornaments.

Circular Necklace

MATERIALS
clear shrink plastic

scissors

hole punch

paintbrush

acrylic paint (Each design was made using a single base
color—violet or green—that was then mixed with white,
grey, or black paint to create gradations of the hue.)

acrylic varnish

suede cord

HOW TO
1. Cut concentric circles from sheets of shrink plastic.

2. Punch a hole centered about ¼" from the top of the largest circle. Use this hole as a guide to line up and punch the holes in the other circles.

3. Bake circles, following the package instructions. Flatten the circles under a heavy book or object while still warm, if necessary.

4. Paint the rough side of each circle. Lighter colors may require two coats. Once dry, add a coat of varnish to seal. Let varnish dry thoroughly.

5. Set circles on top of each other from largest to smallest; thread cord through all the holes.

6. Line up the ends of the cord with circles at the fold. Tie an overhand knot about 1" from the circles. Extra cord in the loop between the plastic circles and knot keeps the circles flat rather than fanning out. Tie another knot at the ends to complete the necklace.

Reindeer Necklace

MATERIALS
clear shrink plastic
ruler
scissors
Christmas stamp
low-tack tape
fine-point permanent marker
hole punch
ribbon

HOW TO
1. Cut shrink plastic to size of the Christmas stamp.
2. Tape shrink plastic to stamp, shiny side out.
3. Trace the stamp image on the shiny side of shrink plastic using the marker.
4. Remove the plastic from stamp and color in the traced image on the rough side with the pen.
5. Punch hole ¼" from top center of design.
6. Bake, following package instructions; let cool, and add ribbon.

9. *For the Little People (or the Child at Heart)* WINTER WILDLIFE SNOW GLOBES

These mesmerizing miniature worlds are simple to make and can be geared to the holiday or a recipient's hobby or passion depending on the figurines you select.

MATERIALS
plastic figurines—deer, penguins, polar bear, etc.
waterproof glue
faux ice cubes
glass jar with tight-fitting lid
distilled water
white or silver glitter
glycerin

HOW TO
1. Glue figurine(s) to faux ice cubes; let dry.
2. Glue figurine(s)/ice cubes to underside of jar lid; let dry completely.
3. Working over a sink, pour distilled water to the top of jar.
4. Add a spoonful of glitter and a few drops of glycerin.
5. Invert the figurine assembly into the water and screw the lid in place. (Give it a shake; you may need to add more water or glitter to your liking.)
6. Before turning over snow globe, seal lid with glue to make sure it doesn't leak.

10. *For the Romantic*
ETCHED SNOWFLAKE HURRICANES

MATERIALS

computer and printer

printable adhesive paper or plastic (8½" x 11")

3 to 4 glass hurricanes in multiple sizes

craft knife

chemical-resistant gloves and goggles

small paintbrush

glass-etching cream

glass cleaner

sponge

HOW TO

1. Download free Christmas font at www.dafont.com (we used two different snowflakes in two different sizes).

2. Print snowflakes on adhesive paper.

3. Place printed paper on hurricane, working from the middle out to smooth bubbles.

4. With craft knife, cut out snowflakes.

5. Once area has been cut out, peel away the cutouts.

6. With a paintbrush, dab a generous amount of etching cream on exposed glass, making sure it doesn't seep underneath paper.

7. Follow instructions for leave-on time (approximately 10 to 15 minutes).

8. Wash off cream, gently rubbing away the excess with a soft sponge.

9. Peel away the adhesive paper to reveal the design.

Handcrafted CONFECTIONS

Making treats is an age-old holiday tradition. From fudge to truffles to brittle, you'll find a recipe for every sweet tooth on your list.

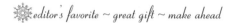

editor's favorite ~ great gift ~ make ahead

Ambrosia Truffles

Makes about 3 dozen • Hands-On Time: 25 min. • Total Time: 3 hr., 25 min.

Grand Marnier spikes these buttery bites. Count on them going fast at party time.

  6 Tbsp. whipping cream
  3 (4-oz.) white chocolate baking bars, finely chopped
  3 Tbsp. butter
  2 Tbsp. orange liqueur
  ⅓ cup finely chopped dried pineapple
  ¾ cup sweetened flaked coconut, toasted
  ¾ cup finely chopped pecans, toasted

1. Bring whipping cream to a simmer in a small heavy saucepan over medium heat. Remove from heat; add white chocolate, butter, and liqueur, stirring until smooth. Stir in pineapple.
2. Pour white chocolate mixture into an 8-inch square baking dish; cover and chill 2 hours or until firm.
3. Shape white chocolate mixture into 1-inch balls. Combine coconut and pecans; roll balls in coconut mixture. Place truffles on a wax paper-lined baking sheet. Cover and chill 1 hour or until firm. Store in an airtight container up to 2 weeks.

Note: We tested with Ghirardelli White Chocolate Baking Bars.

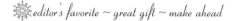

editor's favorite ~ great gift ~ make ahead

Black and White Peppermint Fudge

Makes 2 lb. • Hands-On Time: 25 min. • Total Time: 1 hr., 25 min.

Layers of dark and white chocolate give chocolate lovers the best of both worlds. A sprinkling of chopped chocolate-covered mints adds the crowning touch. Substitute red and white peppermint candies to get our cover look.

  2 cups miniature marshmallows
1¾ cups sugar
  ¼ cup butter
  Pinch of salt
  1 (5-oz.) can evaporated milk
  ¾ cup bittersweet chocolate morsels
  ½ teaspoon peppermint extract
  ¾ cup white chocolate morsels
 12 miniature chocolate-covered peppermint patties, chopped

1. Combine first 5 ingredients in a large heavy saucepan. Cook over medium heat, stirring constantly, until mixture comes to a boil. Boil 6 minutes, stirring constantly. Remove from heat; pour half of mixture into a small bowl.
2. Add bittersweet morsels to half of marshmallow mixture, stirring until morsels melts. Stir in peppermint extract. Spread mixture into a buttered 8-inch square pan.
3. Stir white chocolate morsels into remaining half of marshmallow mixture, stirring until morsels melt. Pour mixture over chocolate layer in pan. Sprinkle chopped candies over white chocolate layer. Cover and chill 1 hour or until firm. Cut fudge into squares.

Black and White Peppermint Fudge

Dark Chocolate Mint Buttons

 *great gift ~ make ahead*

Dark Chocolate Mint Buttons

Makes 2 dozen • Hands-On Time: 30 min. • Total Time: 4 hr., 42 min.

Three easy recipes combine to make a decadent dark chocolate cookie with a luscious mint filling.

CHOCOLATE COOKIES
½ cup butter, softened
⅓ cup powdered sugar
¾ cup all-purpose flour
¼ cup Dutch process cocoa
¼ tsp. baking powder
⅛ tsp. salt
½ tsp. peppermint extract

MINT FILLING
¼ cup butter, softened
2 cups powdered sugar
1½ Tbsp. crème de menthe
Green liquid food coloring (optional)

COATING
1 (12-oz.) package dark chocolate morsels
Wax paper

1. Prepare Chocolate Cookies: Beat butter at medium speed with an electric mixer until creamy; gradually add powdered sugar, beating well.
2. Combine flour, cocoa, baking powder, and salt; gradually add to butter mixture, beating at low speed after each addition. Stir in peppermint extract.
3. Shape dough into a 9-inch log; wrap in wax paper, and chill 4 hours. Or wrap and freeze in a zip-top plastic freezer bag up to 1 month.
4. Preheat oven to 350°. Cut dough into ⅜-inch slices, and place 1 inch apart on lightly greased baking sheets. Bake at 350° for 10 to 12 minutes or until set. Cool on baking sheets 2 minutes; transfer to wire racks, and cool completely (about 10 minutes).
5. Meanwhile, prepare Mint Filling: Beat butter at medium speed with an electric mixer until creamy; gradually add powdered sugar, beating well. Add crème de menthe, beating just until blended. Stir in 1 drop food coloring, if desired.
6. Spoon Mint Filling into a zip-top plastic freezer bag (do not seal). Snip 1 corner of bag to make a small hole. Pipe about 1 tsp. frosting onto each cookie.

7. Prepare Coating: Microwave chocolate morsels in a medium-size, microwave-safe bowl at HIGH 50 seconds to 1 minute or until melted, stirring after 30 seconds. Stir until smooth. Spoon chocolate over cookies, 1 at a time, coating tops completely; place on a rack over waxed paper, flat side down, until coating is set (about 15 minutes).. Store in an airtight container up to 1 week.

 *great gift ~ make ahead ~ quick & easy*

Doughnut Chips

Makes 16 servings • Hands-On Time: 7 min. • Total Time: 7 min.

Glazed doughnuts are transformed into an addictive crisp snack, thanks to a panini press.

8 glazed doughnuts

1. Preheat panini press. Using a serrated knife, cut doughnuts in half horizontally.
2. Place doughnut halves, cut sides up, in batches, in a pre-heated lightly greased panini press. Cook 1 to 2 minutes or until browned; transfer doughnut chips to a wire rack to cool completely. (Chips will crisp as they cool.) Store in an airtight container up to 1 week.

Cinnamon Sugar Doughnut Chips: Sprinkle doughnut halves, cut sides up, with cinnamon sugar before closing panini press to cook. Proceed with recipe as directed.

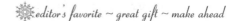*editor's favorite ~ great gift ~ make ahead*

Chocolate Chip Cookie Mounds

Makes 1½ dozen • Hands-On Time: 30 min. • Total Time: 11 hr., 5 min.

Baking these little gems from the frozen state helps preserve their shape. Wait 'til you bite into one of these crisp cookies with a meltaway middle!

  1 (16½-oz.) package refrigerated chocolate chip cookie
     dough
  ¼ cup all-purpose flour
  1 (11-oz.) bag milk chocolate kisses
  Parchment paper
1½ (7-oz.) milk chocolate candy bars, broken
  1 Tbsp. shortening
  Wax paper

1. Place cookie dough in a bowl; add flour, kneading until blended. Divide dough into 20 (1¼-inch) balls. Gently push a chocolate kiss into center of each dough portion; reshape each into a ball. Place on a jelly-roll pan; freeze 1 hour. Transfer cookie balls to a large zip-top plastic freezer bag; freeze 8 hours.
2. Preheat oven to 350°. Place frozen cookie balls on a parchment paper-lined large baking sheet.
3. Bake at 350° for 12 to 13 minutes. Cool on pan 5 minutes; transfer to wire racks, and cool completely (about 15 minutes).
4. Microwave chocolate bars and shortening in a small microwave-safe glass bowl at MEDIUM (50% power) 1½ to 2 minutes; stir until smooth. Quickly dip each cookie into melted chocolate. Let harden on wax paper (about 1 hour).

Note: We tested with Hershey's Meltaway Kisses (not the classic Hershey's Kisses).

*great gift ~ make ahead ~ quick & easy*

Not Your Grandma's Divinity

Makes about 1 lb. • Hands-On Time: 9 min. • Total Time: 17 min.

Grandma can still make divinity in her trusty heavy pan, but you can turn out the same pillowy-soft candy in half the time using your microwave.

  2 cups sugar
  ½ cup light corn syrup
  2 egg whites
  1 tsp. vanilla extract
  Wax paper

1. Stir together sugar, corn syrup, and ⅓ cup water in a 3-quart microwave-safe bowl. Cover with plastic wrap; microwave at HIGH 3 minutes. Uncover, and microwave at HIGH 6 to 7½ minutes or until mixture begins to turn light brown around edges.
2. Meanwhile, beat egg whites at high speed with an electric mixer until stiff peaks form (about 4 minutes).
3. Using oven mitts, pour hot sugar mixture in a thin stream over beaten egg whites, beating at high speed. Add vanilla, and beat just until mixture holds its shape (about 3 to 4 minutes). Working quickly, drop divinity by rounded Tbsp. onto wax paper.

Pecan-Orange Divinity: Stir in ½ cup toasted chopped pecans and 1 tsp. orange zest after adding vanilla. Proceed with recipe as directed. Makes about 1 lb.

Note: We tested divinity using an 1100-watt microwave oven and a KitchenAid mixer. We recommend using the mixer's wire whisk attachment for beating the egg whites to stiff peaks, and then switching to the paddle attachment while continuing to beat until candy holds its shape.

Not Your Grandma's Divinity

Pistachio-Cranberry
Brittle

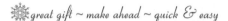 *great gift ~ make ahead ~ quick & easy*

Pistachio-Cranberry Brittle

Makes 2¾ lb. • Hands-On Time: 4 min. • Total Time: 16 min.

We think this is one of the best microwave-made candies to date. The results deliver a pretty candy that's nutty and crunchy.

- 2 cups sugar
- 1 cup light corn syrup
- 1 cup pistachios, toasted
- 1 cup sweetened dried cranberries
- 3 Tbsp. butter, cut into pieces
- 1 tsp. baking soda
- 1 tsp. vanilla extract

1. Stir together sugar and corn syrup in a large microwave-safe bowl. Cover with plastic wrap, and microwave at HIGH 4 minutes.

2. Uncover, and microwave at HIGH 7 to 8 more minutes or until mixture is light golden brown; stir in pistachios and cranberries. Microwave, uncovered, at HIGH 1 minute or just until mixture returns to a boil.

3. Using oven mitts, remove bowl from microwave. Quickly stir in butter, soda, and vanilla. (Candy will foam.)

4. Quickly pour candy mixture onto a buttered 15- x 10-inch jelly-roll pan or large baking sheet, spreading to edges of pan using buttered metal spoons or spatulas. Cool completely. Break candy into pieces. Store in an airtight container.

Pumpkin Seed Brittle: Substitute 1 cup shelled, roasted, and salted pumpkin seeds (pepitas) for pistachios and cranberries. Stir in pumpkin seeds after first 4 minutes of cooking. Proceed with recipe as directed, microwaving at HIGH 7 to 8 minutes in step 2. Makes about 1½ lb.

Note: We tested brittle using an 1100-watt microwave oven.

 *great gift ~ make ahead*

Chocolate-Dipped Candied Orange Peel

Makes ¾ lb. • Hands-On Time: 27 min. • Total Time: 4 hr., 27 min.

Use this pretty citrus peel to decorate a holiday cake or chop it and sprinkle over ice cream or pudding.

- 3 large navel oranges
- 4 cups sugar, divided
- 1 (12-oz.) package semisweet chocolate morsels
- 3 Tbsp. shortening

1. Using a sharp, thin-bladed knife, cut a ¼-inch slice from each end of oranges.

2. Place flat-end down on a cutting board, and remove peel in strips, cutting from top to bottom following the curvature of fruit. Remove any bitter white pith from peel. Cut peel into ¼-inch-thick strips. (Reserve orange flesh for another use.)

3. Place orange peel strips in a large saucepan with cold water to cover. Bring to a boil over high heat. Reduce heat; boil 5 minutes; drain. Repeat procedure twice.

4. Combine 3 cups water and 3 cups sugar in saucepan; add orange peel. Bring to a boil; reduce heat, and simmer, uncovered, 2 hours or until peel is tender and translucent. Drain. Using small tongs or a fork, arrange peel in a single layer on wire racks; dry at least 2 hours. Toss peel in remaining 1 cup sugar.

5. Microwave chocolate and shortening in a medium-size, microwave-safe bowl at HIGH 1 minute, stirring after 30 seconds. Stir until smooth. Carefully dip candied orange peel halfway in chocolate. Return to wire racks, and dry completely. Store in an airtight container.

❋ editor's favorite ~ great gift ~ make ahead

Sea Turtles

Makes 2½ dozen • Hands-On Time: 25 min. • Total Time: 55 min.

One key to success in making these scrumptious turtle candies is finding a rimmed pan large enough to hold four cups of pecans spread in a single layer.

- 4 cups chopped pecans
- 2 (11-oz.) packages caramel bits
- ¼ cup heavy cream
- 2 tsp. vanilla extract
- 2 (4-oz.) bittersweet chocolate baking bars, chopped
- ¼ cup shortening, divided
- 2 (4-oz.) white chocolate baking bars, chopped
- 2 Tbsp. coarse sea salt (optional)

1. Preheat oven to 350°. Bake pecans in a single layer in a 15- x 10-inch jelly-roll pan 5 to 6 minutes or until toasted and fragrant, stirring halfway through. Cool completely.

2. Melt caramel bits and cream in a heavy saucepan over medium heat, stirring until smooth. Remove from heat; stir in vanilla.

3. Using 1 Tbsp. caramel mixture at a time, spoon circles close together over pecans, covering entire pan. Chill 10 minutes or until caramel is firm. Carefully lift candies, and transfer to a serving platter, reserving remaining pecans in pan. Redistribute pecans on pan into a solid single layer. Repeat procedure with remaining caramel mixture, spooning circles over remaining pecans.

4. Meanwhile, microwave bittersweet chocolate and 2 Tbsp. shortening in a small microwave-safe bowl at HIGH 30 seconds or until melted. Stir until smooth. Repeat procedure with white chocolate and remaining 2 Tbsp. shortening. Stir until smooth. Spoon 1 Tbsp. chocolate (either bittersweet or white) onto each caramel turtle candy. Sprinkle lightly with salt, if desired. Let candies harden at room temperature or in refrigerator.

Spoon circles of the warm caramel over the pecans until the pan is covered. Chill to firm then lift candies from pan.

Top half of the candies with the melted bittersweet chocolate-shortening mixture and half with the white-chocolate-shortening mixture.

Toasted Hazelnut
Fudge

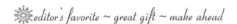

Toasted Hazelnut Fudge

Makes 2 lb. • Hands-On Time: 11 min. • Total Time: 1 hr., 11 min.

There's no denying the glorious hazelnut flavor in this easy-to-make decadent candy.

    1 (14-oz.) can sweetened condensed milk
    1 (11.5-oz.) package bittersweet chocolate morsels
    ½ cup hazelnut spread
    1 cup chopped toasted hazelnuts
    1 tsp. vanilla extract
    Pinch of salt

1. Grease bottom of an 8-inch square pan. Line bottom and sides of pan with aluminum foil, allowing 2 to 3 inches to extend over sides. Butter foil. Set pan aside.
2. Combine first 3 ingredients in a large heavy saucepan. Cook over medium heat until melted and smooth, about 8 minutes, stirring occasionally. (Mixture will be thick.) Remove from heat; stir in hazelnuts, vanilla, and salt. Spoon fudge into prepared pan. Cover and chill 1 hour or until firm.
3. Lift from pan, using foil sides as handles. Cut fudge into small squares.

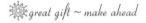

Bittersweet Chocolate Bourbon Balls

Makes 5½ dozen • Hands-On Time: 29 min. • Total Time: 8 hr., 49 min.

These giftables have creamy centers and flecks of toasted pecans. Place the confections in candy cups, and give them in a gift box.

    ½ cup butter, softened
    2 (16-oz.) packages powdered sugar
    ½ cup bourbon
    1 cup chopped pecans, toasted
    12 oz. bittersweet chocolate, chopped
    3 Tbsp. shortening

1. Beat butter at medium speed with an electric mixer 2 minutes or until creamy. Gradually add powdered sugar and bourbon; beat 1 to 2 minutes or until smooth. Stir in pecans.

2. Shape mixture into 1-inch balls. Microwave chocolate and shortening in a medium-size, microwave-safe bowl at HIGH 1 minute, stirring after 30 seconds. Stir until smooth.
3. Dip bourbon balls in chocolate, and place on a wax paper-lined baking sheet. Let stand 8 hours or until set.

German Chocolate Cracker Candy

Makes 2¾ lb. • Hands-On Time: 3 min. • Total Time: 1 hr.

Speed up prep for this decadent break-apart candy by popping the finished pan of treats into the refrigerator to firm up the chocolate.

    2 sleeves chocolate graham crackers (18 whole crackers)
    2 cups firmly packed light brown sugar
    1 cup unsalted butter
    2 (4-oz.) sweet baking chocolate bars, chopped
    ⅔ cup milk chocolate morsels
    ¾ cup coarsely chopped natural almonds (with skin) or pecans, toasted
    1 cup unsweetened coconut flakes

1. Preheat oven to 350°. Arrange graham crackers snugly in a single layer, slightly overlapping, on a parchment paper-lined 15- x 10-inch jelly-roll pan.
2. Heat brown sugar and butter in a saucepan over medium heat until melted and smooth, about 5 minutes. Pour sugar mixture over crackers.
3. Bake at 350° for 15 minutes; reduce oven temperature to 325°, and bake 10 more minutes. Remove from oven; sprinkle with chocolates. Let stand 10 minutes; gently spread chocolate over crackers. Sprinkle with nuts and coconut; press gently to adhere. Chill 20 to 30 minutes or until hardened. Break candy into pieces. Store in an airtight container.

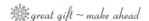
great gift ~ make ahead

Rudolph's Reindeer Crunch

Makes 17 cups • Hands-On Time: 17 min. • Total Time: 2 hr., 32 min.

Use two jelly-roll pans or shallow roasting pans to bake this big-yield snack mix.

- 12 cups popped popcorn
- 1½ cups salted mixed nuts
- ½ cup butter
- 2 cups firmly packed brown sugar
- ¼ cup light corn syrup
- ¼ tsp. salt
- 1 tsp. vanilla extract
- 1 (12-oz.) package white chocolate morsels
- Wax paper
- 1 (12-oz.) package semisweet chocolate morsels

1. Preheat oven to 250°. Combine popcorn and nuts in a large bowl; set aside.

2. Melt butter in a large heavy saucepan. Stir in brown sugar and next 2 ingredients; bring to a boil over medium heat, stirring constantly. Boil 5 minutes, stirring occasionally. Remove from heat; stir in vanilla. Pour sugar mixture over popcorn mixture; stir until coated.

3. Spread mixture in a single layer on 2 lightly greased shallow roasting pans or 17- x 12-inch jelly-roll pans. Bake at 250° for 45 minutes, stirring every 15 minutes. Cool in pans on wire racks 15 minutes. Divide mixture into thirds.

4. Microwave white chocolate morsels in a microwave-safe bowl at HIGH 1 minute, stirring after 30 seconds. Pour melted white chocolate over one-third of popcorn, tossing to coat. Transfer to wax paper, and cool completely. Repeat melting procedure with semisweet chocolate, and stir into another one-third of popcorn. Transfer to wax paper, and cool completely. Once chocolate popcorns have hardened, toss with remaining one-third plain popcorn. Store in an airtight container.

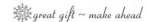
great gift ~ make ahead

Buttery Almond Toffee

Makes about 2½ lb. • Hands-On Time: 5 min. • Total Time: 1 hr., 19 min.

Here's a pure and simple microwave toffee recipe. This is one you and your friends will make again and again. Don't limit yourself to almonds—crack open your favorite nut and experiment with countless creations.

- 1 cup chopped whole natural almonds (with skin)
- 2 Tbsp. unsalted butter
- 1 cup unsalted butter
- 2 cups sugar
- ¼ cup light corn syrup
- ½ tsp. salt
- 1 tsp. vanilla extract
- Parchment paper
- 1 (12-oz.) package semisweet chocolate morsels

1. Preheat oven to 350°. Combine almonds and 2 Tbsp. butter on a jelly-roll pan. Bake at 350° for 8 minutes; stir and bake 2 more minutes. Drain on paper towels.

2. Place 1 cup butter in a large microwave-safe bowl. Cover with plastic wrap, and microwave at HIGH 1 minute. Add sugar, ¼ cup water, corn syrup, and salt. Cover and microwave at HIGH 3 minutes. (This step washes down sugar crystals from sides of pan.) Uncover, stir gently, and microwave at HIGH 10 minutes or until golden.

3. Using oven mitts, remove bowl from microwave; stir in vanilla. Pour candy mixture, without scraping sides of pan, onto a greased baking sheet lined with parchment paper, quickly spreading candy to ¼-inch thickness.

4. Sprinkle chocolate morsels over toffee; let stand 1 minute or until chocolate begins to melt. Spread chocolate evenly over candy; sprinkle with almonds, pressing gently with fingertips. Cool completely. Chill 1 hour or until firm. Break toffee into pieces. Store in an airtight container.

Coffee Toffee: Combine 1½ tsp. instant espresso powder with ¼ cup water when adding water as recipe directs. Cook candy mixture in microwave at HIGH as recipes directs above, microwaving only 9 minutes (instead of 10) at the end of step 2. One-half cup chopped chocolate-covered coffee beans can be sprinkled over melted chocolate topping. Makes about 2 lb.

Note: We tested toffee using an 1100-watt microwave oven.

Buttery Almond Toffee

Road Trip to Grandma's,
page 28

Love It? GET IT!

Many items pictured in the book are one-of-a-kind or no longer available—we've listed similar looks when possible. Source information is current at the time of publication. If an item is not listed, its source is unknown.

• page 13—**mugs:** Sagaform, www.sagaform.com/usa, (856) 626-1340

• page 17—**glass vase:** A'Mano, Birmingham, AL, (205) 871-9093, www.amanogifts.com

• pages 18-19—**pumpkins:** Myers Plants and Pottery, Pelham, AL, (205) 663-6597, www.myersplantsandpottery.com; **pottery:** Tena Payne, (205) 702-7055, www.earthbornpottery.net; **glassware and linens:** At Home, Birmingham, AL, (205) 879-3510, www.athome-furnishings. com; **flatware:** Pottery Barn, (888) 779-5176, www.potterybarn.com

• pages 21-27—**pottery:** Tena Payne, (205) 702-7055, www.earthbornpottery. net and Table Matters, Birmingham, AL, (205) 879-0125, www.table-matters.com

• pages 36-37—**mercury glass:** At Home, Birmingham, AL, (205) 879-3510, www.athome-furnishings.com

• page 52—**pewter bowl and ornaments:** Attic Antiques, Birmingham, AL, (205) 991-6887

• page 53—**molds:** Attic Antiques, Birmingham, AL, (205) 991-6887; **vases:** Barbara Eigen, A'Mano, Birmingham, AL, (205) 871-9093 www.eigenarts.com, www.amanogifts.com; **decorative balls:** At Home, Birmingham, AL, (205) 879-3510, www.athome-furnishings.com

• pages 54-55—**towels:** Attic Antiques, Birmingham, AL, (205) 991-6887; **canisters and pitchers:** Tricia's Treasures, Birmingham, AL, (205) 871-9779; **silver ornaments, button trees and garland:** Ballard Designs, (800) 536-7551, www.ballarddesigns.com; **paper clock:** Rosegate, (205) 980-5014, www.therosegate.com

• page 56—**wine charms and stirrers:** Pier 1 Imports, www. pier1.com; **Frostie drinks:** Cost Plus World Market, www.worldmarket.com

• page 60—**blue glass vases:** Leaf & Petal, Birmingham, AL, (205) 877-3030, www.leafnpetal.com; **assorted birds:** Leaf & Petal, Old Time Pottery, www.oldtimepottery.com, Flowerbuds, Inc., Birmingham, AL, (205) 970-3223, www.flowerbudsinc.com

• page 61—**stockings:** A'Mano, Birmingham, AL, (205) 871-9093, www.amanogifts.com; **snowballs:** Leaf & Petal, Birmingham, AL, (205) 877-3030, www.leafnpetal.com; **painting:** Claire Cormany, (205) 249-5585, www.clairecormany.com

• page 62—**candleholders:** Pottery Barn, (888) 779-5176, www.potterybarn.com; **metal garland:** Gold Leaf Designs, (877) 738-1790, www.goldleafdesigngroup.com

• page 64—**painting:** Helen DeRamus, Griffith Art Gallery, (205) 985-7969, www.griffithartgallery.com; **candles:** Christine's, Birmingham, AL, (205) 871-8297

• pages 66-67—**vases and silver balls:** Gold Leaf Designs, (877) 738-1790, www.goldleafdesigngroup.com

• page 68-69—**flower box and test tube vases:** Gold Leaf Designs, (877) 738-1790, www.goldleafdesigngroup.com

• page 70—**cups:** Rachel Dormer Ceramics, www.racheldormorceramics.com

• page 73—**trees and mercury glass votives:** Tracery Interiors, Birmingham, AL, (205) 414-6026, www.traceryinteriors.com

• pages 74-75—**ornaments:** Tracery

Interiors, Birmingham, AL, (205) 414-6026 , www.traceryinteriors. com; **china:** Bromberg & Co., Inc., Birmingham, AL, (205) 871-3276, www.brombergs.com

• page 76—**china:** L'Objet "Aegean" in platinum, Bromberg & Co., Inc., Birmingham, AL, (205) 871-3276, www.brombergs.com

• page 77—**green china:** Phillippe Deshoulieres "Arcades"; **red china:** Hermes "Balcons du Guadalquivir"; **gold china:** Pickard "Auratus"; all from Bromberg & Co., Inc., Birmingham, AL, (205) 871-3276, www.brombergs.com

• pages 78-79—**flatware:** Alain Saint-Joanis "Soliman," Bromberg & Co., Inc., Birmingham, AL, (205) 871-3276, www.brombergs.com

• pages 80-81—**wire snowflakes:** Flowerbuds, Inc., Birmingham, AL, (205) 970-3223, www.flowerbudsinc.com; **cards:** Night Owl Paper Goods, (205) 868-1619, nightowlpapergoods.com; **metal diamond-shaped card holder:** Willow House, www.willowhouse.com

• pages 82-83—**wreath gift-toppers:** At Home, Birmingham, AL, (205) 879-3510, www.athome-furnishings.com; **tree ornament gift-topper:** Lamb's Ears Ltd. Birmingham, AL, (205) 969-3138, www.lambsearsltd.com

• page 85—**wooden spoons:** Anthropologie, (800) 309-2500, www.anthropologie.com

• pages 86-87—**wreaths:** Davis Wholesale Florist, Birmingham, AL, (205) 595-2179, www.daviswholesaleflorist.com

• page 89—**Christmas tree wreath:** Davis Wholesale Florist, Birmingham, AL, (205) 595-2179,

www.daviswholesaleflorist.com

• page 97—**sangria glasses:** Table Matters, Birmingham, AL, (205) 879-0125, www.table-matters.com; **embroidered napkins:** Table Matters, Birmingham, AL, (205) 879-0125, www.table-matters.com

• page 97—**plaid china plate:** Jeffrey Banks, www.jeffreybanksdesign.com

• pages 102-103—**bird place card holder and napkin ring:** Table Matters, Birmingham, AL, (205) 879-0125, www.table-matters.com

• page 108—**compote:** Table Matters, Birmingham, AL, (205) 879-0125, www.table-matters.com

• page 110—**bird votives:** Leaf & Petal, Birmingham, AL, (205) 877-3030, www.leafnpetal.com

• pages 114-115—**polka dot napkin and silver tree:** Table Matters, Birmingham, AL, (205) 879-0125, www.table-matters.com

• page 117—**white artificial trees:** Table Matters, Birmingham, AL,

(205) 879-0125, www.table-matters.com

• page 121—**red plate:** A'Mano, Birmingham, AL, (205) 871-9093, www.amanogifts.com

• page 124—**white plate with paper plate look:** Barbara Eigen, A'Mano, Birmingham, AL, (205) 871-9093 www.eigenarts.com, www.amanogifts.com

• page 126—**napkin:** Table Matters, Birmingham, AL, (205) 879-0125, www.table-matters.com

* *

Thanks to these CONTRIBUTORS

Thanks to these Birmingham businesses

A'Mano
Anthropologie
At Home
Attic Antiques
Ballard Designs
Barbara Eigen
Bromberg & Co., Inc.
Claire Cormany
Cost Plus World Market
Davis Wholesale Flowers
Doug Davis
Flowerbuds, Inc.
Gold Leaf Designs
Jeffrey Banks Design
Lamb's Ears, Ltd.
Leaf & Petal
Myers Plants and Pottery
Night Owl Paper Goods
Old Time Pottery
Pier 1 Imports
Pottery Barn
Rachel Dormer Ceramics
Rosegate
Table Matters
Tena Payne at Earthborn Pottery
Tracery Interiors
Tricia's Treasures
Willow House

Thanks to the following homeowners

Kay Clarke
Katherine & John Cobbs
Missie & Sims Crawford
Rebecca & Ben Fulmer
Ashley & Ken Polk
Susan & Jeff Ray
Jan & Kyle Ware

GENERAL INDEX

METRIC EQUIVALENTS

The recipes that appear in this cookbook use the standard U.S. method for measuring liquid and dry or solid ingredients (teaspoons, tablespoons, and cups). The information in the following charts is provided to help cooks outside the United States successfully use these recipes. All equivalents are approximate.

Metric Equivalents for Different Types of Ingredients

A standard cup measure of a dry or solid ingredient will vary in weight depending on the type of ingredient. A standard cup of liquid is the same volume for any type of liquid. Use the following chart when converting standard cup measures to grams (weight) or milliliters (volume).

Standard Cup	Fine Powder (ex. flour)	Grain (ex. rice)	Granular (ex. sugar)	Liquid Solids (ex. butter)	Liquid (ex. milk)
1	140 g	150 g	190 g	200 g	240 ml
¾	105 g	113 g	143 g	150 g	180 ml
⅔	93 g	100 g	125 g	133 g	160 ml
½	70 g	75 g	95 g	100 g	120 ml
⅓	47 g	50 g	63 g	67 g	80 ml
¼	35 g	38 g	48 g	50 g	60 ml
⅛	18 g	19 g	24 g	25 g	30 ml

Useful Equivalents for Dry Ingredients by Weight
(To convert ounces to grams, multiply the number of ounces by 30.)

1 oz	=	¹⁄₁₆ lb	=	30 g
4 oz	=	¼ lb	=	120 g
8 oz	=	½ lb	=	240 g
12 oz	=	¾ lb	=	360 g
16 oz	=	1 lb	=	480 g

Useful Equivalents for Length
(To convert inches to centimeters, multiply the number of inches by 2.5.)

1 in			=	2.5 cm		
6 in	=	½ ft	=	15 cm		
12 in	=	1 ft	=	30 cm		
36 in	=	3 ft	= 1 yd =	90 cm		
40 in			=	100 cm	=	1 m

Useful Equivalents for Liquid Ingredients by Volume

¼ tsp			=		1 ml	
½ tsp			=		2 ml	
1 tsp			=		5 ml	
3 tsp	=	1 Tbsp	=	½ fl oz	15 ml	
		2 Tbsp	= ⅛ cup =	1 fl oz	30 ml	
		4 Tbsp	= ¼ cup =	2 fl oz	60 ml	
		5⅓ Tbsp	= ⅓ cup =	3 fl oz	80 ml	
		8 Tbsp	= ½ cup =	4 fl oz	120 ml	
		10⅔ Tbsp	= ⅔ cup =	5 fl oz	160 ml	
		12 Tbsp	= ¾ cup =	6 fl oz	180 ml	
		16 Tbsp	= 1 cup =	8 fl oz	240 ml	
		1 pt	= 2 cups =	16 fl oz	480 ml	
		1 qt	= 4 cups =	32 fl oz	960 ml	
				33 fl oz	1000 ml	= 1 l

Useful Equivalents for Cooking/Oven Temperatures

	Fahrenheit	Celsius	Gas Mark
Freeze water	32° F	0° C	
Room temperature	68° F	20° C	
Boil water	212° F	100° C	
Bake	325° F	160° C	3
	350° F	180° C	4
	375° F	190° C	5
	400° F	200° C	6
	425° F	220° C	7
	450° F	230° C	8
Broil			Grill

RECIPE INDEX

Twelve Ways at Christmas,
page 80

Holiday PLANNER

When the leaves fall and weather turns brisk, it's time to start planning for the holidays. From decking your halls to opening your doors to friends and family, our helpful planner makes getting organized a cinch. Save it so you can refer to it when making next year's plans.

NOVEMBER *2011*

Sunday	Monday	Tuesday	Wednesday
		1	2
6	7	8	9
13	14	15	16
20	21	22	23
27	28	29	30

Thursday	Friday	Saturday
3	4	5
10	11	12
17	18	19
Thanksgiving 24	25	26

Go Green

As you deck your house in festive red and green this holiday season, take a step further and go green with your decorating and entertaining.

- When buying a clothing gift, opt for organic cotton. Grown and processed without the use of toxic chemicals, it's eco-friendly and wonderfully soft next to your skin.
- Before you leave to visit relatives, turn off the lights and unplug any chargers not in use, such as cell phones and laptops, which still use about 5 watts per hour when they aren't recharging a battery.
- Try to buy local for this year's holiday feast. For your presentation, attach cards to dishes naming ingredients' origins, crediting the cheese plate to a local dairy or cool-season herbs to your own container garden.
- Give a gift that requires no wrapping at all—a donation to a favorite local charity, which is good for the environment as well as the community.
- All the prep work in the kitchen leaves tons of fruit and vegetable scraps that you can use to start composting. Get started by finding out more at www. composting101.com
- Reusable bags aren't just for the grocery store. Buy a chic bag and bring it to the mall, which will also help you keep up with all your purchases.
- Don't throw your Christmas tree to the curb. Have it turned into mulch. To find a Christmas tree-recycling program in your area, visit www.earth911.org.

DECEMBER *2011*

Sunday	Monday	Tuesday	Wednesday
4	5	6	7
11	12	13	14
18	19	20	21
Christmas 25	26	27	28

Thursday	Friday	Saturday
1	2	3
8	9	10
15	16	17
22	23	Christmas Eve 24
29	30	New Year's Eve 31

Cookie Baking Tips

- Measure liquid ingredients in a glass measuring cup. Spoon solids into metal or plastic measuring cups.
- Pack brown sugar firmly into dry measuring cups for an accurate measurement.
- Coat a glass measuring cup with cooking spray for easy removal of syrups.
- Before cutting bar cookies, harden them in the freezer.
- Use shiny baking sheets; dark pans absorb more heat and can cause overbrowning.
- Start your holiday baking with fresh boxes of baking soda and baking powder.
- Coat knife or scissors lightly with flour before chopping candied fruits.
- Grate fruit rind with a zester plane found at most cooking shops.
- Store nuts in plastic freezer bags in the freezer for a longer shelf life.
- Vanilla candy coating (commonly referred to as almond bark) can be found in the baking section of grocery and crafts stores.
- Store baked and cooled cookies in airtight containers. Line bottom with aluminum foil, plastic wrap, or wax paper. Separate each layer with aluminum foil or wax paper. Seal container, and label with contents and date before freezing.
- Most cookie doughs can be tightly wrapped and stored in the refrigerator up to one week or in the freezer up to three months.

Decorating PLANNER

List the finishing touches that you need to trim a picture-perfect house this season.

Decorative materials needed

from the yard ....

....

from around the house..

....

from the store..

....

other..

Holiday decorations

for the table ....

....

for the door ....

....

for the mantel ....

....

for the staircase..

....

other..

Holiday Meal-Preparation Tips

The secret to a successful meal begins with the right ingredients and equipment. Take the time to plan your menu and organize your schedule to ensure great results.

• Perfect Planning

Your oven will get more use in the next two months than any other time of the year. Learn how to organize your menu and juggle recipes so everything comes out hot and on time.

Once you've decided on your menu, think through how to cook it. If all of your dishes have to go in the oven—and at different temperatures and times—you might have trouble. Modify your menu so that you get the turkey done first; then choreograph the rest of your prep time so that all your dishes come out together.

• Turkey Tricks

It can take two to three days to thaw a frozen turkey in the refrigerator. So, buy it ahead of time while the selection is still good, and plan when and how you'll thaw it. Find defrosting charts attached to the turkey, or visit www.butterball.com.

After the turkey thaws, stick your hand into the cavity and pull out the neck and giblets. They're usually wrapped in paper. If you forget this step and find these after you've finished cooking, your turkey is still safe to eat; just pull 'em out, enjoy a laugh, and go on.

Once you remove the turkey from the oven, cover it loosely with foil to allow the bird to rest. The juices absorb back into the turkey, and it carves easily. This resting is prime oven time for additional casseroles or dessert.

• Gadgets to Get:
- Bulb baster
- Turkey lifters
- Timer
- Thermometer
- Roasting racks
- Cheesecloth
- Oven mitts

Take the Holiday Party OUTSIDE

It's time to hang stockings, roast marshmallows, and reminisce by the fire. Everything doesn't always have to happen indoors. Move the decorations outside to play up great views, and the party will be sure to follow. This is a real bonus when the space indoors is tighter than a minivan headed to grandma's house.

• Cute-as-Can-Be Conifers

A dwarf Alberta spruce placed in a copper pot makes a good balance for a bigger tree inside. Burlap-wrapped false cypresses and cedars do double duty, serving as decorations and then going home with guests when the party is over. Just let folks know that, after the holidays, these little guys will gladly spend winter outdoors in a pretty pot.

• "Plumb" Pretty Bows

You can make a shiny red bow from an unlikely material: plumbing strapping! Found at hardware stores everywhere and costing less than $2 a roll, it's the best "ribbon" for making an outdoor bow. True, fabric may be easier to handle, but, once you know a few tricks, this bow isn't hard to make and can be reused for years to come. Spray-painted a high-gloss red, it can be used alone, on a container such as a galvanized bucket, or with greenery.

• Metal Bows Made Easy

1. Wearing gloves, cut 5 feet of plumbing strapping with wire snips. Loop strapping back and forth to form a figure 8, holding the center between your thumb and index finger.
2. Insert 8 inches of wire through the two center holes in the strapping, and twist to secure.
3. Repeat process with a second 5-foot length of strapping. Place sets on top of one another so they make an X, and wire them together well. (This two-part method is a lot easier than handling all of the strapping at once.)
4. Open loops, and bend as needed to form the bow. End pieces can be wrapped around a broom handle to make spirals. Spray-paint with a high-gloss enamel in a well-ventilated area, and allow to dry.

• Magnificent Mossy Stockings

Santa would be sorely disappointed to come down this chimney and not find stockings hung with care. Fashion weather-tolerant booties from chicken wire and then cover with assorted mosses. Sprigs of holly and nandina berries provide the finishing touches. Because the stockings are three-dimensional, they can be filled with goodies.

1. Make a stocking form from chicken wire. Wearing gloves and using a pair of wire snips, cut a 24- x 24-inch square of chicken wire, and fold it in half. Eight inches from the bottom, on the unfolded side, cut out a 5-inch V. Fold the top two-thirds around (folding one raw edge to the inside and the other back around to the outside to form a cylinder). Secure by twisting closed the raw edges of wire using the tip ends of the wire snips or a pair of pliers. Overlap the edges of the bottom one-third of cut wire to form the toe and heel of the boot. Secure using the same method.
2. Use a hot glue gun to attach moss to the chicken wire. A hot-melt glue gun works best for this project because it offers more holding power. Start at the top, and work down. We used Spanish moss for the cuff and alternated bright green reindeer moss and dark green decorative sheet moss for the stripes, finishing the toe and heel with Spanish moss. Berries and variegated holly can be added too. Can't find the moss you want? Spray-paint what you can get in your yard or from a crafts store.

• Spruce Up by the Curb

Tired of the simple red bow adorning the mailbox? This year, give it the royal treatment with festive elements from the yard. Head out on a scavenger hunt for evergreens and berries.
1. Soak a caged block of florist foam. Secure it to the mailbox with wire. Don't worry about the exposed wires; the greenery will mask them. Add materials such as magnolia, boxwood, aucuba, and branches of evergreen to the florist foam. (Tip: Check with the local tree lot for discarded branches and tree trimmings to use in arrangements.) For a dramatic effect, place long pieces of silvery elaeagnus in the mix. Next, tuck in holly or nandina berries for a burst of red. Top it all off with a brilliant red bow. The arrangement will last several weeks outdoors if the florist foam is kept moist.

Party PLANNER

Make sure your party plans stay on point with this time-saving menu chart.

guests	what they're bringing	serving pieces needed
....	☐ appetizer ☐ beverage ☐ bread ☐ main dish ☐ side dish ☐ dessert	....
....	☐ appetizer ☐ beverage ☐ bread ☐ main dish ☐ side dish ☐ dessert	....
....	☐ appetizer ☐ beverage ☐ bread ☐ main dish ☐ side dish ☐ dessert	....
....	☐ appetizer ☐ beverage ☐ bread ☐ main dish ☐ side dish ☐ dessert	....
....	☐ appetizer ☐ beverage ☐ bread ☐ main dish ☐ side dish ☐ dessert	....
....	☐ appetizer ☐ beverage ☐ bread ☐ main dish ☐ side dish ☐ dessert	....
....	☐ appetizer ☐ beverage ☐ bread ☐ main dish ☐ side dish ☐ dessert	....
....	☐ appetizer ☐ beverage ☐ bread ☐ main dish ☐ side dish ☐ dessert	....
....	☐ appetizer ☐ beverage ☐ bread ☐ main dish ☐ side dish ☐ dessert	....
....	☐ appetizer ☐ beverage ☐ bread ☐ main dish ☐ side dish ☐ dessert	....
....	☐ appetizer ☐ beverage ☐ bread ☐ main dish ☐ side dish ☐ dessert	....
....	☐ appetizer ☐ beverage ☐ bread ☐ main dish ☐ side dish ☐ dessert	....
....	☐ appetizer ☐ beverage ☐ bread ☐ main dish ☐ side dish ☐ dessert	....
....	☐ appetizer ☐ beverage ☐ bread ☐ main dish ☐ side dish ☐ dessert	....
....	☐ appetizer ☐ beverage ☐ bread ☐ main dish ☐ side dish ☐ dessert	....
....	☐ appetizer ☐ beverage ☐ bread ☐ main dish ☐ side dish ☐ dessert	....

Party Guest List

Pantry List

Party To-Do List

Christmas Dinner PLANNER

You and your holiday celebration will stay organized with the menu, to-do list, and guest list in our handy meal planner.

Menu Ideas

....
....
....
....
....
....
....

Dinner To-Do List

....
....
....
....
....
....

Christmas Dinner Guest List

....
....
....
....
....
....
....
....
....

Mix-and-Match MENUS

Menus below are based on recipes in the book.

SUPPER BY THE SEA
GINGER-CRANBERRY MOJITO (12x) (PAGE 94)

SEAFOOD APPETIZER TRIO (PAGE 20)

MIXED GREENS SALAD

WILD SALMON PARCELS WITH DILL-SHALLOT BUTTER
(PAGE 106)

MINI MACADAMIA-COCONUT CREAM PIES (PAGE 121)

SEA TURTLES (PAGE 162)

Serves 12

SPECIAL OCCASION SOIREE
LEMON BASIL MARTINIS (2x) (PAGE 97)

STEAK AU POIVRE WITH COGNAC MUSHROOMS (3x) (PAGE 103)

HERBED POMMES ANNA (2x) (PAGE 113)

GLAZED VEGETABLES WITH PARSLEY (PAGE 24)

CHOCOLATE-PRALINE SUNDAE SHOTS (PAGE 115)

Serves 12

DOWN-HOME DINNER WITH A TWIST
APPLE TEA PUNCH (PAGE 116)

BRUSSELS SPROUTS WITH SPICY PECANS (2x) (PAGE 108)

WHITE CHEESE GRITS WITH MUSTARD GREENS AND BACON
(PAGE 44)

FIG-GLAZED HAM (PAGE 103)

PECAN PIE COBBLER WITH HONEY ICE CREAM (PAGE 27)

Serves 12

VERY MERRY MEAL
POINSETTIA SANGRIA (2x) (PAGE 119)

GREEN BEANS WITH FRIED SHALLOTS (PAGE 24)

BROWNED-BUTTER GLAZED CARROTS (PAGE 44)

MAPLE-BRINED TURKEY BREAST WITH CURRANT-STUFFED
BAKED APPLES (PAGE 107)

LITTLE GINGERBREAD SCONES (PAGE 120)

Serves 12

CHIC LADIES' LUNCH
SPIKED SATSUMA CHAMPAGNE (PAGE 39)

HAM-WRAPPED OLIVE SHRIMP (PAGE 99)

SWEET POTATO SALAD (PAGE 33)

MINI HERBED FRITTATAS WITH SMOKED SALMON AND CRÈME FRAÎCHE
(PAGE 99)

LEEK AND WILD RICE TART (PAGE 111)

MAPLE-WALNUT BLONDIE STACKS (PAGE 118)

Serves 8

COZY BRUNCH
MERRY MIMOSAS FOR A CROWD (2x) (PAGE 10)

EXTREME HOT CHOCOLATE (PAGE 129)

COUNTRY HAM ROLLS WITH ORANGE MUSTARD (PAGE 98)

POPPY SEED-LEMON PANCAKES (2x) (PAGE 126)

SPINACH-ARTICHOKE STRATA (2x) (PAGE 14)

FRESH FRUIT

Serves 12

Gifts AND *Greetings*

Keep up with relatives' sizes, jot down gift ideas, and record purchases in this convenient chart. Also use it to add to your ever-growing Christmas card list.

Gift List and Size Charts

name /sizes	gift purchased/made	sent/delivered

name ....

jeans_____ shirt_____ sweater_____ jacket_____ shoes_____ belt_____

blouse_____ skirt_____ slacks_____ dress_____ suit_____ coat_____

pajamas_____ robe_____ hat_____ gloves_____ ring_____

name ....

jeans_____ shirt_____ sweater_____ jacket_____ shoes_____ belt_____

blouse_____ skirt_____ slacks_____ dress_____ suit_____ coat_____

pajamas_____ robe_____ hat_____ gloves_____ ring_____

name ....

jeans_____ shirt_____ sweater_____ jacket_____ shoes_____ belt_____

blouse_____ skirt_____ slacks_____ dress_____ suit_____ coat_____

pajamas_____ robe_____ hat_____ gloves_____ ring_____

name ....

jeans_____ shirt_____ sweater_____ jacket_____ shoes_____ belt_____

blouse_____ skirt_____ slacks_____ dress_____ suit_____ coat_____

pajamas_____ robe_____ hat_____ gloves_____ ring_____

name ....

jeans_____ shirt_____ sweater_____ jacket_____ shoes_____ belt_____

blouse_____ skirt_____ slacks_____ dress_____ suit_____ coat_____

pajamas_____ robe_____ hat_____ gloves_____ ring_____

name ....

jeans_____ shirt_____ sweater_____ jacket_____ shoes_____ belt_____

blouse_____ skirt_____ slacks_____ dress_____ suit_____ coat_____

pajamas_____ robe_____ hat_____ gloves_____ ring_____

name ....

jeans_____ shirt_____ sweater_____ jacket_____ shoes_____ belt_____

blouse_____ skirt_____ slacks_____ dress_____ suit_____ coat_____

pajamas_____ robe_____ hat_____ gloves_____ ring_____

Christmas Card List

name	address	sent/delivered

HOLIDAY *Memories*

Cherish your holiday for years to come with handwritten recollections of this season's memorable moments.

Treasured Traditions

Keep track of your family's favorite holiday customs and pastimes on these lines.

....

....

....

....

....

....

....

....

....

....

....

....

....

Special Holiday Activities

What holiday events do you look forward to year after year? Write them down here.

....

....

....

....

....

....

....

Holiday Visits and Visitors

Keep a list of this year's holiday visitors. Jot down friend and family news as well.

....
....
....
....
....
....
....
....
....
....
....
....
....
....
....
....
....
....
....
....
....
....
....
....
....
....

This Year's Favorite Recipes

Appetizers and Beverages ....
....
....
....
....
....

Entrées ....
....
....
....

Sides and Salads ....
....
....
....

Cookies and Candies ....
....
....
....

Desserts ....
....
....
....

Looking AHEAD

Holiday Wrap-up

Use this checklist to record thank-you notes sent for holiday gifts and hospitality.

name	gift and/or event	note sent
		☐
		☐
		☐
		☐
		☐
		☐
		☐
		☐
		☐
		☐
		☐
		☐
		☐

Notes for Next Year

Write down your ideas for Christmas 2012 in the lines below.